BILLY DRAKE
FIGHTER LEADER

BILLY DRAKE
FIGHTER LEADER

THE AUTOBIOGRAPHY OF
GROUP CAPTAIN B. DRAKE
DSO, DFC & BAR, DFC (US)

WITH CHRISTOPHER SHORES

GRUB STREET · LONDON

Published by
Grub Street
The Basement
10 Chivalry Road
London SW11 1HT

Copyright © 2002 Grub Street, London
Text copyright © 2002 Billy Drake and Christopher Shores

British Library Cataloguing in Publication Data
Drake, Billy
  Billy Drake, Fighter Leader: the autobiography of
  Group Captain B. Drake, DSO, DFC & Bar, US DFC
  1. Drake, Billy 2. Fighter pilots – Great Britain – Biography
  3. World War, 1939-1945 – Personal narratives, British
  I. Title II. Shores, Christopher, 1937-
  90.5′44941′092

ISBN 1 902304 97 7

Typeset by Pearl Graphics, Hemel Hempstead

Printed and bound in Great Britain by
Biddles Ltd, Guildford and King's Lynn

CONTENTS

INTRODUCTION

Like many an aviation enthusiast, I came to 'know' Billy Drake initially when reading Paul Richey's seminal work, *Fighter Pilot*, which I purchased as a paperback in 1955. As my interest in fighter pilots and my research associated with them grew, I began to realise that here was one of the true 'greats' of the RAF in World War II . So I wanted to know more. *Tiger Squadron*, the account of 74 Squadron's exploits in both wars written by that great old fighter ace of the first war, Ira 'Taffy' Jones, and published in 1954, included a list of Fighter Command fighter pilots with more than 12 victories by 30 June 1941, in which Billy's name did not appear (the cut-off date was too early for that), although he was mentioned therein, and indeed his picture appeared, sitting next to 'Taffy' in a group at 53 OTU.

The first breakthrough occurred for me in 1956 with the chance purchase of the *Daily Mail Quiz Book Number 2 – Aircraft*. Inside this rather unlikely publication, was a list of Leading British Fighter Pilots – World War II, and there at No. 11 on the list was Wing Commander B. Drake, DSO, DFC & Bar, DFC (US), listed with 24 victories. As others produced autobiographies, or had their stories written for them, no word of Billy appeared. There were articles in that wonderful magazine, *RAF Flying Review* – but none about him. Who was he? What had he done after his time with 1 Squadron?

Two events occurred almost simultaneously to provide the answers. Firstly, someone in *Air-Britain* tipped me off to look at decoration citations in the wartime issues of the *London Gazette*, whilst in 1962 E.C.R. Baker's book, *The Fighter Aces of the R.A.F.* included a chapter about Billy, called *Shark Leader*. There it was! A synopsis of his career, and an indication of where I should look when I began the serious research for my first book, *Aces High*, two years later. Much of this early lack of information probably derives from Billy's long absence in Portugal, for it was at this very point that he left the Royal Air Force and disappeared. Thus as I began to meet more and more of the RAF's fighter pilots, Billy was one who was to remain something of an enigma to me for many further years.

After writing about him in the original volume of *Aces High*, published in 1966, and in *Fighters over the Desert* (1969), it was not until the early

1990s that I finally had the great pleasure and privilege of meeting him, following his return to live once again in London. Even then, his logbooks, medals, and other memorabilia were lost, or spread around the world. Consequently, it was not until after the revised edition of *Aces High* (1994) and its addendum Volume 2 (1999) had been published, that I felt I had been able to do proper justice to his achievements.

Persuading him to consider preparation of his autobiography was a different matter however, for he had for many years resolutely avoided doing so, or allowing any biography to be written about him. Whilst he is undoubtedly a great 'kidder' with a rather wicked sense of humour, he is essentially a most modest man. It therefore took a lot of work to convince him that the interest existed, not just in the war years, but in his whole career and in the story of his life to warrant such a venture. He was most concerned not to produce, as he put it, "just another 'There I was, upside down, with nothing on the clock'" story.

When it was explained to him that there would also be considerable interest in what he had to say about the people he had known, served and flown with, he was at pains to stress that he would not wish to record anything which might hurt or annoy those still living.

My promises of help and support, coupled with the guidance that John Davies at Grub Street was able to offer, caused his resolve to waver, and finally to collapse, followed by his agreement that this book might proceed. Over the past two years Billy and I have become frequent companions, with long sessions of memory-jerking discussions regarding the many personalities he knew, and journeys through his logbooks, which fortuitously reappeared from within the family, being interspersed with pleasant meals and talk about the fundamentals of life.

In being allowed to help Billy Drake in the preparation of this auto-biography, I feel I have been deeply privileged. I am honoured to have been associated with so great a warrior, and gratified beyond words to have become his friend, which I very much hope I shall always remain.

In conclusion it needs to be said that, whilst his recall of the years up to his departure from the RAF were sufficiently well-recorded to maintain their chronological integrity, some of the events associated with his long, and frequently traumatic periods in Portugal, may not have occurred in precisely the order in which they now appear. Memory here was not aided to the same extent by forms of written evidence.

Further, whilst I have little doubt from our conversations that some of Billy's adventures of a more amorous nature may be considered to have been legion, his innate gentlemanliness has protected the ladies involved from mention or identification.

Christopher Shores
Sherborne, Dorset, March 2002

CHAPTER 1

EARLY YEARS

I have few particular memories of my early childhood, although it could certainly be classed as far from the ordinary. My father, Dennis John Drake, was a direct descendant of Sir Francis – he of the bowls on Plymouth Ho! before sailing out to defeat the Spanish Armada. Father had been born at Ashe House, the family home in Devon, and was to qualify as a doctor at Barts Hospital, where a fellow student was Conan Doyle (later Sir Arthur, creator of Sherlock Holmes). During the First World War father became an Army doctor, and whilst so employed met and married my mother in London. I was the fruit of their union, born on 20 December 1917, and christened Billy – not William.

Mother had been born Gerda Browne, one of fifteen children of an Irish Catholic family living in Australia. She had obtained a job as a nanny/childrens' nurse in Ceylon, but had travelled to England with the family for which she worked at the outbreak of war in 1914. Her father – my maternal grandfather – had obviously been something of an adventurer. Prior to leaving his native isle, he had risen to become head of all the lightships around Southern Ireland. However, he subsequently emigrated to Australia settling in Queensland during the period of gold rush fever, and went to work in the goldfields.

His early efforts brought success, and he was able to amass quite a quantity of gold. But these were wild and lawless times, and he was knocked on the head and lost the lot . . . back he went and mined some more, which this time he was to hang onto. With the proceeds of his labours he then purchased a schooner, using this to trade between Australia and New Zealand. Sadly, I never had the chance to know him, for during a very bad storm the mainmast of his vessel was blown down, landing on him and killing him.

My own father remained a somewhat remote figure to me, and I never got to know him well. Certainly he was slightly eccentric and above all, loved to travel. As an infant I was taken out to Australia, and then to Fiji for about 18 months, whilst he practiced medicine in both locations. We then returned to England, but father's next venture was to open an English clinic in Tangiers. It was at this stage that I commenced my schooling, which was to follow a somewhat erratic path. As I recall, I was a fairly placid child until roused, whereupon I became something of a demon. Volatile is perhaps the word! At each of my first two schools it seems that some classmate managed to rile me, and from each I was expelled for beating up my tormentor. These proved to be the original examples of a degree of fighting ability and belligerency which would come to the fore later. Ultimately I found myself in the French Lycée in Tangiers until we returned to England again.

Here I was despatched to a day school in Stroud, where my father had purchased a practice, but rapidly the same thing happened, and my parents were requested to remove me. Father (who was not a Catholic) now succumbed to my mother's blandishments and agreed that a Catholic establishment might provide the necessary discipline to bring me into line. So I was sent to Prior Park at Bath, a preparatory school run by the Christian brothers. There was little Christian charity or brotherly love here – they were in my opinion (and experience) a sadistic bunch of buggers as far as I was concerned.

I remember well that I became a member of the choir, possessing for a time quite a nice soprano voice – until this began to break with the onset of puberty and adolescence. The 'understanding' of my predicament by Brother Burke was to administer two strokes with a leather strap. I was mortified and never forgot it, yet when I visited the place years later and reminded him of his cruelty, the old devil didn't even remember the event. It was probably all part of the day's work as far as he was concerned.

I do recall especially being rather horrified by the details of Spanish history which we were taught, and particularly by the details of the Inquisition, all of which was rather rammed down our throats by the brothers. Certainly it had a quite profound and detrimental effect on any respect or affection which I might otherwise have retained for the Roman Catholic religion.

As an only child I spent a great deal of time on my own, and cannot recall being particularly happy, or of having any fond memory. I was very much a complete and utter loner, and perhaps because of this I was a late starter in almost everything. I certainly was never an intellectual thinker at this time – at least, not consciously. It was undoubtedly also a lonely business being caught between two religions, which at that time remained quite deeply hostile towards each other.

I had been given a bicycle, and would frequently go off on my own, riding for miles when at home in the holidays. My parents had very much the old Victorian attitude that children were best seen but not heard, and I must say that they did not seem to be in the least interested as to where I was or what I was doing, as long as I kept out of trouble. In my travels I spent a lot of time visiting castles and the like, and developed a fondness for old buildings and history.

Despite the general apparent lack of any particular parental interest or guidance in my development, my father did me one great service as it was to transpire. He taught me how to use a shotgun from the age of twelve, explaining particularly the art of deflection shooting. I was to maintain my interest in such shooting for many years, seeking out clay pigeon shooting ranges whenever I could find them. I shall mention later the extent to which this training would benefit me in years to come.

As I approached the age to be despatched to my senior school, my parents argued over whether I should go to father's old school, Uppingham, or to the Catholic-run Downside, favoured by mother. Strangely, I was asked what I felt about the matter, and I had some quite different ideas of my own. I had recently been skiing, and much enamoured of this sport, suggested that I might instead be sent to a school in Switzerland. Somewhat to my surprise my parents agreed, and I entered the Kollegium Maria Hilf, a strict premier boarding school run by Swiss German Catholics in Schweitz, where I began learning German very rapidly.

This was, of course, now the early 1930s; a time when Fascism and National Socialism were beginning to make themselves felt in much of Europe. Those pupils at the school, who were not Swiss Germans, were either from Germany itself, or were Italians, all of whom were becoming embued with the spirit of Mussolini and Adolf Hitler. As the only English boy in the school, I became the butt of repeated slurs and criticism of the British Empire – a situation of which I rapidly tired.

On return home for the holidays I therefore looked out my boxing gloves, having done some boxing earlier in my education, and returned to Schweitz determined to put a stop to this. Initially, I enlisted the support of my housemaster, explaining the situation to him and advising that I intended to challenge to a boxing match anyone who referred unflatteringly to me or my country from then on. I asked that he be prepared to act as referee – a role to which he somewhat bemusedly agreed. During the next few weeks I fought 12 bouts, most of which I lost, although I did enjoy one success against an opponent who was smaller, fatter, and Italian – but it did the trick, and thereafter I was left in peace.

After two years at the Kollegium I moved to a French Swiss school in Geneva, the Institute Florimont, where I improved my French to add to my linguistic abilities. I remained there for a year and then, with my secondary education effectively complete, I returned home, where for the next nine months I did very little but loll around.

What followed was to bring me once more into conflict with my parents. As a small boy I had visited Alan Cobham's Flying Circus on one of its 'barnstorming' visits to the area where we lived. I had obtained a 20-minute flight for half a crown (12.5 new pence). From that moment I had wanted to fly and had devoured books on the fliers of World War 1. I also regularly spent my pocket money on that wonderful magazine *Aeroplane*.

At this stage my parents were trying to persuade me to a career of their choice or approval – although the options suggested were quite wide, including becoming a doctor, a diplomat, a hotelier – indeed anything that was not connected with flying, which they were dead against.

It was at this stage, with nothing decided, that I found in the latest copy of *Aeroplane*, an advertisement – seeking applicants for a short service commission in the Royal Air Force. The term in question was to be of four years duration, and a terminal gratuity of £300 was offered. At first my parents were united in their adamant opposition to such an idea, but my own misreading of the advertisement came strangely to my assistance. I had read the gratuity to be an annuity, and laboured to them how advantageous this annual sum could prove to be in the rest of my life!

When they read the advertisement, my error was spotted at once: "The boy is not just stupid, he is a moron!" they decided. This would settle the matter once and for all. Let him go to the Air Ministry for an interview, for he would be certain to be turned down when he showed such ignorance of the English language.

So by this turn of events, I received the necessary parental permission to travel to London for the interview, where to my delight and their amazement and chagrin, I was accepted. But there was a snag for initially I failed the medical, my eyesight proving not to be of a high enough standard. However, I was not just turned away, for the doctor advised that he believed this was not an inherent defect, but was probably caused by reading at night in a bad light. I should therefore report back for a further eye test three months later.

For the next three months I religiously avoided reading in anything but the best of illumination and when I presented myself again – now nearly 18 years old – I was in.

CHAPTER 2

TRAINING DAYS

So there I was, a somewhat naïve and unworldly young man – indeed, little more than a boy – about to enter my chosen profession! I was still only at the minimum age acceptable for the grant of a short service commission – 17 years and nine months. But the offer had been made and readily accepted, and off I was to go to Air Service Training at Hamble, on the Hampshire coast in the south of England, not so far from Southampton. My stay here was to be of two months duration for 'ab initio' training at what was still basically a civilian flying school. No uniforms and drill just flying.

My main instructor was one Flight Lieutenant Figgins, who sadly I recall only as a complete nonentity. I also received some instruction from Lord Hamilton, brother of a Scottish laird, who would subsequently fly over Mount Everest in a specially converted Westland Wapiti. I note from my logbook however, that he did not actually fly with me. Many years later he would fly out to Africa to pick up his son, who had also become a noted aviator, and who had been forced to come down there. In so doing, my mentor crashed and was killed.

The aircraft on which we were instructed at Hamble was the Avro Cadet – a smaller version of the RAF's standard trainer of the day, the Tutor. Indeed, I believe that Hamble was the only centre to be equipped with these pleasant little aircraft. I flew several, but G-ACCJ and G-ACNF seem to have been the most frequently inhabited by me.

My first flight at AST was made on 14 July 1936, and following a pre-solo test of some ten minutes by Flying Officer Knocker on 27th of that month, I went off for my first solo – all of 15 minutes on my own. I wish I could say that it was a seminal moment in my life, but I do not recall it being such. Yes, I was pleased, but at the time no more than that.

Thereafter another six weeks or so followed during which I learned to spin the aircraft and undertake various other aerobatics; to restart the propeller in the air, and of course, the obligatory cross-country flights, undertaken on 14 and 18 August – the first to Yatesbury and back, the second to Filton. With 60 hours of flying under my belt – and in my logbook – half of it solo, and a massive five and half hours on instruments, I was passed out as 'Average' on 3 September and was sent off on my first leave.

Partly this was to allow me to arrange my kitting out, for which the princely sum of £50 was provided. Oh how times have changed. For this amount I was able to purchase everything required – uniforms, mess kit, camping equipment, shirts, ties, socks, and shoes – the lot, all purchased at the old Army & Navy Store in Victoria Street, Westminster.

These two weeks were followed by a brief stay at RAF Uxbridge, where we new Acting Pilot Officers on Probation were taught to march and salute, and generally to comport ourselves as officers and gentlemen. From Uxbridge I was posted to 6 Flying Training School at Netheravon in the Salisbury Plain area of Wiltshire. Here it was that my real RAF service commenced. 6 FTS was commanded by Group Captain App-Ellis, reputedly a balloon pilot during the First World War. The school was equipped mainly with various Hawker biplane types, which still provided a sizeable part of the equipment of the RAF's first line squadrons at this time. Training started on the Hart (T), and I made my first flight in K4948 on 22 September 1936 as passenger to my new instructor, Flight Lieutenant Hicks. Happily, I established an immediate rapport with Hicks, and being taught by him proved to be a pleasure; I was able to record my first solo on the Hart on 7 October.

Living now in the Netheravon Officers' Mess, I shared a room with a Romanoff – a Russian émigré in the RAF. I was not to keep in touch with him, but think I recall him running the Parachute School at Ringwood when war broke out. I was however, still very much the loner, and made few friends at 6 FTS. Initially I purchased a motorcycle for 30/- (£1.50 in today's currency), but found this too wet and cold as winter approached. It was therefore replaced by an Armstrong Siddley motorcar for £5. Its condition was not of the best – and it proved necessary to carry two five-gallon drums of oil at all times. Such a consumption of lubricant not surprisingly produced clouds of smoke, and my arrivals and departures must have resembled those of the Demon King!

The next three months passed fairly uneventfully. Besides the flying, we were instructed in various ground subjects at which I was not particularly good – but how I loved the flying. My moment of nemesis almost arrived on New Year's Day, 1937, however. On that memorable date I was given my Chief Instructor's Flying Test – and I failed it. Hicks had demonstrated to me how slowly the Hart could be flown, and had but I realised it, taken the aircraft to its limit in this regard in so doing. I – arrogant young puppy that I was – determined to demonstrate to Squadron Leader Toogood that I could fly the Hart even more slowly than my instructor. On the point of stalling, Toogood snatched the controls from me, opened the throttle, and landed. He then turned to me with the ominous words: "I want to speak to you!" I was failed ignominiously.

Fortunately, I was handed back to Hicks, who personally passed me on 9 January, and I was granted my "Wings". With my flying time now up to 138 hours I was over the second hurdle, still classified as 'Average', and again was sent on leave.

On my return I left the Harts and Audaxes behind, moving to 'D' Flight, the Advanced Training Squadron. In practice, there was to be more flying in both types – but now my main mount became the Hawker Fury. I made my first flight in this beautiful and classic biplane fighter on 2 February 1937. From the same stable as the aircraft I had so recently been flying, there were many similarities – but as a single-seater it was nicer to fly, being faster and more nimble. I was impressed with it, and enjoyed flying it. Here my main instructors were Sergeants Markwick and Webb.

Again however, the period left me with few outstanding memories, as we just got on with the training. I do recall that one day I looked up and saw a most unusual aircraft coming in to land, from which a man dressed like a Martian – or a deep-sea diver – climbed out. It was the Bristol 138A, in which Squadron Leader F.R.D. Swain had just established a World Altitude Record of 49,967 feet (15,230 metres) on 28 September 1936, and it was he, in his early pressure suit, who had disembarked. Squadron Leader Swain was soon to re-enter my life in a somewhat different guise however.

My other more notable memory related to 14 May 1937, when, flying Audax K7355 back from camp at Penrhos, grossly overloaded with tools and an airman, I spun in and crashed. Fortunately, no great damage was done, LAC Burrows was unhurt, and I was not even reprimanded – so the overloading cannot have been considered my fault.

By then the course with D Flight was almost finished. It had included two weeks at Armament Practice Camp, learning to fire the guns, and by 19 May I was ready to go to a squadron. Here my luck seemed to be considerably better than that of many in the service, who when given the opportunity to choose the role they aspired to fulfil, invariably received a posting to something less to their taste. In my case, when given the option, I put down "Fighters", and received the ultimate posting – to B Flight of 1 Squadron at Tangmere – on Hawker Furies! But then I suppose I had been trained on fighters, so there was probably some logic in it.

On arrival at Tangmere came another surprise – my new commanding officer was none other than Squadron Leader Swain – he of the altitude record. My flight commander was Flying Officer H.E.C. Boxer, at that time a member of the squadron's outstanding aerobatic team and an ex-Cranwell Sword of Honour. My arrival in 1 Squadron was not to be particularly auspicious, however. Still very young and a late starter in the ways of adult life, I was considerably impressed by the apparent maturity of most of the resident pilots. At that stage I did not drink or smoke, and was still really a slightly idealistic schoolboy at heart, whilst most of my peers were a year or two older, which at that stage of a young man's development can make a big difference. In any event I did not initially get on well with any of them, and I think they probably found me a little prissy at first. I was soon playing rugby for the station, and as I avoided joining in the 'piss-ups' which followed the matches, this hardly increased my popularity. Their attitude seemed to be that they could not be bothered to waste their time on such an unpromising companion, and this worried me at the time. Clearly it was all part of the process of growing up, but at the time I did not know how to handle it, so initially tended to withdraw further into myself, and to behave like a bit of a prig.

I recall well how this situation began to break down after a time. Following one game of rugby, I was finally persuaded to drink four half-pints of beer, one after the other, and was instantly violently sick on the spot. I was clapped on the back, and from that moment on began to be accepted.

At Tangmere at the time, apart from 1 Squadron, was 43 Squadron, similarly equipped with Furies, and 217 (Coastal) Squadron with Ansons. This latter unit had only recently arrived after formation at Boscombe Down a few months earlier, and would ultimately leave us during the summer of 1938. Soon after my arrival, I rose early one morning, walking into the Mess for breakfast at 7.30 a.m. No one was about, apart from one unidentified figure at the table, hidden behind a copy of *The Times*. As I approached I said "Good Morning!" the paper slowly lowered, a bucolic face appeared, and commented; "Chatterbox!" then disappeared again.

I had not been at Tangmere long when the station switched to 'Summer Routine'. Now we rose at 6 a.m., flew all morning and enjoyed the afternoons free. Much time was spent at Ichenor and West Wittering on the Solent, where we had a Mess boat – an 18-foot dinghy with a centreboard. I soon became one of the Flight's aerobatic pilots, available to join the unit's team when required for air shows and the like.

In June we also received a new B Flight commander, Harry Hamilton

Peck. Harry was a member of a distinguished Canadian military family
from Montreal, and had attended his country's military academy. A
little older than most of us, and therefore of greater maturity and
experience, he was dearly loved by us all. Our Adjutant was an
Australian, Flying Officer A.C. Douglas (known as 'Douggie'). On one
occasion three of us, Douggie leading, took off to fly to Northolt, which
is on the edge of West London. On the way back bad weather closed in
as we approached the South Downs. The Number Three aircraft (flown
by a pilot whose name I do not now recall) had made the fundamental
mistake of flying below rather than above the height at which Douggie
was flying. In consequence, as the land below rose higher in the murk,
he hit some trees and crashed. Douggie and I managed to land in a field
quite close by, but by the time we got there the police had already
arrived and there was nothing we could do; he was dead.

About September 1937 1 Squadron was affiliated with a Fairey
Battle-equipped bomber squadron at Harwell, where I made by first trip
as a passenger in one of these ill-conceived single-engined light
bombers on 23rd of that month. At the controls was Squadron Leader
Tuttle, later to become an Air Marshal.

On another occasion I undertook what was termed a 'Battle Climb'
with Teddy Donaldson, at that time the A Fight commander, and leader
of the squadron aerobatic team at the Hendon Air Pageant and the
Zurich International Fighter Meeting that year. The idea was to climb
to maximum altitude as rapidly as possible. As we did so, each of us
became convinced that the other's aircraft was on fire! In fact we were
both experiencing our first sight of contrails, formed by condensation
at about 22,000 feet. This sight was soon to become so commonplace,
but our misinterpretation of the phenomenon illustrates how low were
the altitudes at which service flying generally took place prior to the
arrival of the modern monoplanes which were soon to supersede our
lovely biplanes.

We were also spending much time and effort practising the FAA
(Fighting Area Attacks), which the Air Ministry had designed for the
interception and destruction of hostile bombers infringing the sanctity
of English skies. What a waste of time these were. They were quite
pathetic. The powers-that-be required that the three attacks devised
were all to be undertaken by tight formations of three aircraft in order
to bring the maximum weight of fire to bear on the intruder which they
were intercepting; in reality they were utterly unprepared for the actual
utilisation of fighters against bombers. We all knew that against
opposing fighters we would have to dogfight in the manner learned
during the first war – although when the fast new monoplanes appeared
there were some who doubted that this would still be possible.

However, fighters were not then expected to be our opponents, for the distances to be flown by our more obvious potential enemies – the Germans – appeared too great to envisage their use. Who then anticipated the rapid fall of France?

But the formations we flew in any event were hopeless. No up-to-date thought appeared to have been given to appropriate battle formations such as the Luftwaffe were already perfecting in Spain. For us, until well after the Battle of Britain, Fighter Command still required that we fly the rigid formations of three aircraft in a tight V (vic), with one or two single aircraft weaving behind the main squadron or flight.

We did attend an annual practice camp for a week each summer, in order to gain some practice at firing our guns. This proved to be very much up my street as a result of my early experience of deflection shooting occasioned by my father's teaching, to which I have referred earlier. Now I was able to put this to good use, proving very successful at this particular activity. Indeed, on one occasion I managed to score 99%, which was virtually unheard of.

Whilst we were so engaged, flying formations much more appropriate for an air show than for real operations, Squadron Leader Swain left us, replaced in early 1938 by Squadron Leader I. Anstruther Bertram, an ex-Navy man and a very nice chap. We had also lost our current flight commander, Harry Peck, when during December 1937 he had been killed whilst undertaking aerobatics with two wingmen. Following engine failure, he tried to bale out too low, and that was it for him. His place was taken by Flight Lieutenant P.J. Sanders.

I also note from my logbook that on 19 January 1938 I was flown to Gosport in the station Miles Magister, a trainer employed as a general 'hack', by Pilot Officer Hill. On the return flight however, the aircraft was piloted by one Group Captain Park; this was none other than Keith Park, later to gain great fame and distinction as the commander of Fighter Command's 11 Group during the summer of 1940. At that time he was our station commander at Tangmere. I also recall the reason for those flights; we had been playing High Cockalorum in the Mess the night before and I had fallen flat on my face, doing myself some injury. I had therefore been flown to the Naval hospital just outside Portsmouth for X-rays. I cannot have been too bad however, for I personally flew the old Magister (L5941) to Kenley next day, and was back in my Fury for another battle climb on 24th.

1938 was the year of Munich, and following Prime Minister Chamberlain's return from his meeting with Adolf Hitler, waving his piece of paper which was supposed to guarantee "Peace in our time", there were some immediate and ominous changes in our lives. Clearly the Air Ministry doubted the veracity of that infamous scrap of paper for we went at once onto a war footing. Our aircraft were painted with camouflage colours, and the guns were kept loaded at all times. In rotas the pilots slept in the hangars at night, us one night, 43 Squadron the next, and so on.

At this time the British Air Attaché to Germany visited all RAF stations to give a talk on the capabilities of the Luftwaffe. He and we agreed that the Fury would be quite incapable of doing anything of value against the aircraft which the Luftwaffe now possessed. The only method we could visualise was to ram, and this we were prepared to do if it proved necessary. We were deeply envious of those lucky buggers who had by then received the new breed of monoplane fighters, and with eight machine guns each were clearly a match for anything which might come their way.

Our own wait for re-equipment was not to be too long delayed however – nor was my own capability. At the start of August 1938 my logbook was endorsed to the effect that I had "*completed training in Fighter duties by day and night*", a statement appended and signed by the commanding officer himself. Quite a surprise, as I had flown by night on only a few occasions.

On 29 August I flew a Gladiator for the first time (K7954), but in October it was Hurricanes, not Gladiators, which began to arrive at Tangmere. I had my first experience of flying one on the 19th of that month – and nearly killed myself straight away! Someone else had flown the aircraft before me for 15 minutes on the reserve fuel tank. As I took off, this became empty and the engine cut. Fortunately, I had kept my wits about me, realised what had happened, and switched immediately to the main tank which allowed power to be restored.

On 26 October I flew to Brooklands in our 'hack' Hawker Demon to collect Hurricane L1687 myself. Here I was briefed by test pilot Dickie Reynell – such a charmer! Very sadly this lovely man was to be killed during the Battle of Britain when he got himself attached to 43 Squadron to gain some operational experience.

However, we had our Hurricanes at last, and on 17 November I flew one of our Furies to Peterborough where we were handing them over to the FTS there for training purposes. Thereafter, the Hurricane was our mount, although for some reason on 9 December I flew Gloster Gauntlet K5358, recording that I undertook aerobatics in a gale!

On 11 January 1939 I first had the opportunity to fire the guns of this formidable new fighter – although only four of the eight were loaded. Peacetime economic stringency dies hard. Firing was into the sea. I also climbed to the aircraft's ceiling – 26,000 feet – and undertook some night flying. In March my latest assessment was recorded in my logbook – "*Average as a Fighter Pilot*".

I digress here on the subject of assessments. I was later to learn that no great notice was paid to such classifications, since they represented purely the view of one individual, who might well categorise one pilot as 'above average' or 'below average', whereas one of his peers would make a significantly different judgement. Similarly, in a particularly experienced unit, or one with an unusually high proportion of gifted individuals, a man might appear 'average', who in another unit could well be considered 'above average'. Thus unless one had been consistently assessed as 'above' or 'below' average by a number of different individuals, we were all generally considered to fall within the category of 'average' – a fairly comfortable place to be.

I note that at the end of March 1939 Anstruther Bertram signed my logbook for the last time, and as a wing commander. Promotion took him away from us, to be replaced by Squadron Leader Patrick Halahan – 'The Bull'. Sanders also left us at this time and I never saw or heard of him again.

1 Squadron – The Personalities

As we approached the almost inevitable outbreak of war during 1939, it is worth looking in some depth at the make-up of the outstanding team, which 1 Squadron had become. Of course, much of the ethos was very different in those days when the British 'class system' was still pretty well pre-eminent and 'equality' was still far from being a universally-accepted concept. Despite the lessons of World War I, the Great Depression and the political turmoil throughout much of the world, it was still a period for the likes of us of naivety and of a moral outlook on life, which today may seem a little quaint.

For a start, with the exception of the new CO, who was a rather older man than the rest of us, we were all bachelors together. Sure, we had girl friends, but the emphasis was on the 'friends'. By and large, people simply did not co-habit in those days; indeed, it was still very strongly perceived that 'nice' girls didn't, although how rapidly things were to change under the emotional impact of war!

So in the Officers' Mess we were all 'mates' who were growing into full adulthood and maturity together, and who were about to be thrown into the cauldron of war – our squadron sooner than most.

Quite early in that war one of our pilots, Paul Richey, was to write *Fighter Pilot* which was initially published in September 1941. This was the first autobiographical account of life as a fighter pilot in World War II, and rapidly (and deservedly) became a 'classic', which has been reprinted on numerous occasions since. In the original edition, Paul was constrained by wartime censorship to refer to us all by nicknames, Christian names, or simply by initial letters. Not until 1955 was an edition published which identified us for who we were. I feel sure that the majority of readers interested enough to be reading this book, will also have read *Fighter Pilot* at some time, and will be familiar with the personalities mentioned therein, myself included.

However, again due to wartime restrictions (and indeed, because the book was written so soon after the events it recorded) Paul was able, generally, to do no more than mention the names and the immediate exploits of those of us who entered his narrative. I therefore seek to set out my personal memories and impressions of those men who Paul and I served with in an effort to put a little 'flesh on the skeletons' so to speak, of those appearing in the pages and photographs in *Fighter Pilot*.

Squadron Leader P.J.H. 'Bull' Halahan. As I have already mentioned, he had only joined us as commanding officer during the spring of that momentous year, and we had not got to know him well. One of three brothers in the RAF, I recall that he was a fairly efficient commanding officer. However, as a married man he lived in quarters, rather than with the rest of us in the Mess. Consequently, at the end of the day's duties he usually disappeared home, and my impression was that he took relatively little interest in us beyond that which duty required of him.

Flight Lieutenant 'Johnnie' Walker was the man who I perceived as really running the squadron. The A Flight commander, he was, next to Halahan, the most senior officer in the unit. He appeared to be older and more mature that the rest of us (although clearly there was actually no great difference in terms of years). He was a member of the squadron aerobatic team, and a heavy pipe smoker. Above all, he was a most lovable person, greatly respected by all.

Flying Officer Plinston had become B Flight commander, and was a rather strange and complex character, My main recollection of him was that he had a tendency to get drunk, decide that he did not like someone's face, and hit them. It really was not on to hit a fellow officer in this manner, whatever the provocation – and he was a big chap; anyone who got hit by him really knew it! He was not to stay with us long after we moved to France, after which I lost track of him.

Flying Officer Prosser Hanks would take over B Flight following Plinston's departure. No problems here – Prosser was a popular and well-respected chap, who we were happy to follow either in the air or on the ground.

Pilot Officer 'Boy' Mould was also a lovable chap. He was an interesting mixture of ex-Halton 'Brat' and Cranwell-trained cadet. This had left him with a few chips on his shoulder, suffering still from his awareness of the definite sub-conscious class distinction, which was very much a part of the RAF at that time. He lost these chips in growing up with the squadron.

Talking of chips however, the man with the biggest was undoubtedly **Flying Officer Leslie Clisby**. Clisby was one of our 'colonials', as we termed them. He was a rough old Aussie 'digger', and basically he did not like Poms. He was very particular about who he made friends with – he could be pretty intolerant. However, as long as one was conscious of his feelings on such matters, you couldn't go wrong with him. He and I shared a room for a while and became quite good friends. At the time he just appeared to become one of the average pilots – there was nothing to indicate the brief brilliance he was to show when the time came.

This was not the case with **Flying Officer 'Pussy' Palmer**; he was an enigma to us, for although he was a brilliant pilot, he did not seem to have anything to say for himself. It was impossible at that time to place him in any category as a fighting personality, although in the end he proved that he was probably potentially better than any of us. He was never to be seen without a cigarette either in his mouth or between his fingers. Later, when he was forced to bale out, he was seen still to have a cigarette 'on' whilst floating down!

Flying Officer 'Hilly' Brown was another 'colonial' to us, though a much more genial one than Clisby. He was a Canadian who played ice hockey and was well liked by all. He was also quite well heeled, and was the first chap in the squadron to spend £100 buying a brand new Ford 10 car. Then of course, there was Paul himself – **Flying Officer Paul Richey** – who was in A Flight. I got to know him quite well as we were both Catholics, and had Downside (his old school and almost mine) as a jumping off point. Additionally, we were of similar class backgrounds, which helped. He was a good rugby player and sportsman – very much one of the team – but we all envied him his ability to win girlfriends – he certainly was not shy.

Flying Officer 'Killy' Kilmartin was already well known to us, as he had been serving with 43 Squadron at Tangmere all the time we were there. He joined us in France in November 1939. Slightly older than most of the rest of us, he already had a background of accomplishments and experience of life, having lived in China and had also become a registered jockey. He was to become one of my greatest friends and was to be best man at my wedding. I was to serve with him twice more in the future.

Another who joined us soon after we moved to France was **Bill Stratton**, another 'colonial', this time from New Zealand. I never had the chance to get to know him well, but he fitted in from the start and seemed to fill the pattern of being a 'good egg'. He ended up after the war as Chief of the Royal New Zealand Air Force.

There were also the NCO pilots – Paul made considerable mention of **Sergeant Soper** in *Fighter Pilot*. Here however that class thing really came to the fore. There was a great dividing line between the officers and NCO pilots. We didn't really talk to them, and certainly didn't make buddies of them. Consequently, whilst we had a considerable respect for their professional and technical abilities, we never really got to know them as personalities. That was clearly a great shame, but was simply how it was in those days – the ethos of the times. It was certainly something that changed quite radically as the war progressed – particularly in the Desert. However, apart from saying that they were both excellent pilots, I cannot comment further on either Soper or **Sergeant Berry** who joined us from 43 Squadron just before we went to France.

Another of our NCOs at that time was **'Darky' Clowes**; again I did not really know him then, but I was to get to do so later, after he had been commissioned. I remember particularly that he suffered from a form of 'sleepy sickness', and would on occasion suddenly fall asleep into his soup when at the meal table, or on other similarly inappropriate and embarrassing occasions.

So these then were the 'characters' with whom I would share the opening months of the war, and generally a better crowd I could not have wished for.

CHAPTER 3

WAR

So there it was – German forces had moved into Poland at the start of September 1939. We had already ascertained – as much from the Press as from our own people – that we would be going over to France as soon as hostilities commenced and we had already commenced taking leave of our girlfriends as the international tension rose.

Indeed, during the week or so before the actual declaration, we had been joined at Tangmere by considerable numbers of Reservists, who had been recalled, and by people from the Post Office Telephones, who were to improve our communications network. Already the squadron was fully mobile for the move, amounting to circa 250 men with the necessary transport. Thus it was quite a large unit, which prepared to move to France.

Many of the Reservists were slightly older than us, some having enjoyed a full air force career already. Sadly I have to say again that at this stage, due to the almost total exclusion that rank and class still imposed between those with commissions and those without, we hardly knew the squadron's airmen, be they aircraft ground crews or administrative staff. This situation would, happily, rapidly disappear as the realities of war thrust us all into closer proximity.

This was, of course, very different from the other two services. In both the Navy and the Army, the junior officers at least, lived and operated in close conjunction with the men, who it was their task to lead in battle, be it by land or sea. Here, as John Terraine pointed out in his brilliant book *The Right of the Line*, the air force was totally different. In a squadron such as ours only the officers and a few of the senior NCOs actually did the fighting. The bulk of the personnel were there to service and supply them, but not to take an active part in belligerent activities themselves.

On 3 September 1939 we were all sitting at dispersal at around midday, waiting for something to happen, when the Prime Minister, Neville Chamberlain, came on the radio to tell the nation that a state of war existed between our country and Adolf Hitler's Germany. We were expecting it, of course, and there was neither shock nor euphoria. We quietly wondered how we would react to events and what might happen – although mainly to ourselves; talking about such things was still 'not done'.

In practice, little happened at first. I record flying a "last beat up of the East Coast" on the 6th, and then three days later we flew over to Le Havre, me in my faithful L1687. Here we were to provide cover for the arrival of the British Expeditionary Force as it landed at Cherbourg. We settled in at our new airfield – like Tangmere at that time, of grass. Our Mess at the airfield was a convent, whilst the alternative in town had been a brothel. In both cases the resident ladies had moved out first!

For the next month we saw nothing of note, but enjoyed some excellent French food. At this stage we did not enjoy the benefit of the early warning system, which had been established in Southern England. We were not aware of the existence of radio location (or radar, as it came to be known later in the war), but clearly none was yet available in France. We therefore maintained standing patrols throughout much of the daylight hours, and also practised those ridiculous Fighting Area section attacks supposedly to be employed against enemy bombers.

I recall that it was about Christmas time before we became aware that a proper system of control had been set up – radar must have arrived by then. We were joined by a Plt Off Brown, who later became famous as a Ground Controlled Interception expert.

On 9 October, the BEF having completed its disembarkation, we moved to our designated permanent base at the village of Vassincourt, where our duty was to provide fighter support and defence for the aircraft and airfields of the RAF's Advanced Air Striking Force. At this time this grandly named organisation comprised a number of squadrons of those obsolescent wonders, the Fairey Battle. At our new base we were permitted to take over the local mayor's parlour as our Mess, where we would spend a great deal of time when not flying during the next few months, sitting around a big table, talking, reading, or playing cards. We were billeted out at a variety of local farmhouses etc, which offered accommodation of various levels of 'comfort' or one might say, degrees of squalor! Rapidly, the weather deteriorated as we approached a particularly harsh and bitter winter.

My own accommodation featured a double bed, but so cold and dank was the weather that the bedding seemed permanently damp. In an effort to overcome this, my "landlady" provided me with a heated brick, wrapped in a towel. My foremost memory of that winter still remains of the miserable cold.

There was little to do or see in Vassincourt, and certainly we did not enjoy a high life of socializing and dining. Much time was spent at dispersal, which was housed in a prefabricated hut of 'Nissen' type. Only Paul Richey and I spoke any French, so there was little contact with the local population, who generally tended to keep themselves to themselves. We usually ate in the Mess.

At the airfield we were looked after by the French Pioneer Corps, whilst we were provided with a liaison officer/interpreter. This was Moses Demozay, who seemed to be a nice little man of good breeding, who did his job efficiently. I never got to know him well, though I am aware that following the fall of France, he managed to get to England where he flew Spitfires under the 'nom de guerre' Morlaix. There were, however, rumours that some of the claims he made were of a rather dubious nature.

There was an occasional foray into the nearest town of substance, Bar-le-Duc, to which we were driven, I recall, by one LAC Dunlop. We would visit the local hotel, the Metz et Commerce, run by Madame Jeanne, a most charming lady. The hotel was presided over by her mother who sported an enormous wig. There were some very strange local laws at this time, one of which forbade the drinking of alcohol on certain days. On such occasions, if in town, we sat around drinking very strong coffee, which had been liberally 'laced' with whiskey, brandy, or some other such noxious spirit.

Still we talked of little that was serious. It was frowned upon to talk 'shop' in the Mess, and in typical upper-class British style, religion, politics and sex were 'no-go areas'. The result was that one never got to know one's brother officers in any real depth, as our talk tended to be of sport and irrelevancies. Such operational sorties as we were called upon to make were few and far between. Until we got proper ground control, most were scrambles to pursue contrails at height, which generally could not be caught.

We had got to know our Hurricanes quite well by now, and had great confidence in them, although for a period of about three days at the height of the winter, the oil froze in all of them, and none could be started. At this time Fighter Command had decreed that the guns of our aircraft should be harmonised to provide a 'scatter' pattern of bullets, rather like a shotgun's blast. This refected a lack of confidence in the shooting ability of most pilots, the aim being to ensure that at least some ammunition struck the potential target *somewhere* – the 'barn door' approach . After the initial engagements, some of us realised that this was unlikely to prove very successful in actually bringing down aircraft, rather than just 'peppering' them. Unofficially at first, we had the guns 'spot' harmonised to allow all the fire from our eight guns to meet at one point – usually about 250 yards ahead of us – to bring the greatest possible weight of fire to bear at one point, in order to inflict the maximum damage. Certainly, with my proven skills in air firing, this is something that I personally did at the first opportunity.

On one occasion, for a bit of entertainment, I borrowed a despatch rider's motorcycle and went for a spin. Unfortunately as I came down a hill, I failed to note that there was a hump-backed bridge at the bottom of it. On hitting this, I came off, although luckily for me, I suffered no serious damage. By now we were somewhat disillusioned with our CO, 'Bull' Halahan, who seemed to have deserted us and moved into the much greater comfort of a nearby chateau. It was rumoured that he had fitted himself up not only with warm, comfortable accommodation, but also with some feminine company.

The other fighter squadron of the AASF, No 73, was based some way away, and we rarely saw them. We were visited on occasion by French fighter pilots in their Curtiss Hawks or Morane 406s, but as always, the language problem remained. Generally they lived their own lives, and we did not see a great deal of them. There was certainly little in the way of formal liaison or planning.

At Christmas we all, as I recall, had home leave for the first time. Several of the boys took the opportunity to get married, including Paul Richey, Prosser Hanks and 'Boy' Mould. Quite a lot of us also took short breaks in Paris, where we stayed at the Crillon Hotel and Bar. One of these visits had a profound effect on me, and one, which was to work critically in my favour in the not so distant future.

On one such leave – I think I had gone to the city with Paul – we went to visit a friend of his, the Hungarian couturier, Marjorie Dunton, who had a showroom in the Rue St Honoré. There I met a delightful American girl in uniform. She turned out to be Helen Ahrenfeldt, a daughter of the Ahrenfeldt porcelain concern, which was based in Limoges. Although a US citizen, she was the product of an Irish mother and Swedish father, and was an established artist. With the outbreak of war however, she had joined the American ambulance corps, a voluntary outfit operating in France, and was driving an ambulance with another girl, Polly Peabody of the Peabody Trust in London. Helen and I looked at each other, and it was love at first sight.

During March and April 1940 there was a little more activity as the weather improved, and finally on 19 April I met the enemy for the first time. Several of us had been scrambled after a contrail, but this proved to be an all-blue photographic reconnaissance Spitfire on its way into Germany, and therefore flying at far too great an altitude for us to reach. Nonetheless, whilst in the air we spotted some Messerschmitt Bf 109s and attacked these. In my logbook I noted "*1 Me 109 shot down in Germany & perhaps 1 other*". I later added to this "*1 Me 109 shot down just over the line. 1 Me 109 probably over Metz*".

Available records give a somewhat fuller account of this early engagement, for it appears that four of us encountered nine Bf 109Es from 7 Staffel of Jagdgeschwader 53 near the frontier in the Sierck-les-Bains area. 'Johnnie' Walker claimed one shot down near Thionville, while 'Hilly' Brown claimed a second, which he reported fell on German soil. I attacked three, seeing one go down apparently out of control (the second of the claims I noted in my logbook), and then pursued another into Germany, where I reported that it crashed into a hill. Apparently one Messerschmitt fell in the first encounter, a Leutnant Sievers being killed. A second – I am sure the aircraft I pursued – crash-landed near Gau-Bickelheim, being classed as 50% damaged. He had led me a merry chase at low level, under high-tension cables and over rivers. Eventually, he pulled up and lost speed, allowing me to get a good shot into him and I reported that he appeared to have crashed into a hill. I understand that the pilot claimed that he had come down because he had run out of fuel. I think I helped him – just a little.

But of course, this had been an engagement with fighters, which posed us few problems in the tactical sense. We were still far from certain what we should do if we met bombers, and on a few occasions still practised those ludicrous Fighting Area attacks. Ah, we were soon to learn . . . .

As April turned to May we heard the occasional vague rumours that something might be afoot – but there was no proper briefing or dissemination of intelligence information. With dawn on 10 May we motored up to our airfield – and heard the noise of many German aircraft overhead.

We all got in a couple of sorties during the day, and on one of mine 'Boy' Mould and I shared in shooting down a Heinkel He111 (I am told that this was an aircraft of 5 Staffel, Kampfgeschwader 53). Over the next couple of days or so we operated from a field by a little village called Berry-au-Bac, near Rennes. We had a feeling of total chaos reigning; in and out of our Hurricanes four or five times a day, we seemed to see nothing but German aircraft everywhere.

Referring to my logbook, I see that all the squadron's records of flying times were lost for this period. I thought I had flown until 12 May, but records which are available seem to indicate that I was still around the next day. Certainly I recall setting out with Prosser Hanks and two others to try and protect the Battle attacking the bridges in the Maastricht area, and this must have been on the 12th. All we saw was 10/10ths Bf 109s and we could not do a thing, so we pissed off.

I note that during this period, apart from the shared Heinkel, I also claimed three Dornier Do 17s confirmed and a fourth unconfirmed. It was on 13 May (as I now understand) that I had just set one Dornier in a formation on fire, and was getting behind another, when there was an almighty bang and my Hurricane burst into flames; a Messerschmitt Bf 110 had got onto my tail while I was involved with the bombers, and was still shooting. I didn't like this at all.

Initially I panicked – which probably saved my life, for although I undid the seat harness and got up to get out, I had forgotten to open the cockpit hood. By now I was covered in petrol and glycol, and there were flames everywhere. I finally managed to get the cockpit open, but whilst doing so the aircraft had turned over onto its back. Consequently all the flames, which of course were going upwards, were drawn away from me, and I dropped out of the cockpit and pulled the ripcord. Still the 110 was shooting at me, and then he was past and gone.

As I floated down, I realised that I had been wounded in the back and in one leg although only by splinters as it transpired, not by bullets. I landed in a field, but rapidly discovered that my troubles were by no means over. In those days my hair was very blond; additionally, my eyes are blue, and I was wearing white peacetime overalls. The French farmers who rapidly arrived on the scene, armed with scythes and pitchforks, were initially convinced that I was one of the 'sale boches', and were all set to have a go at me. With a little difficulty I was able to persuade them that I was indeed a 'pilote anglaise', whereupon they all embraced me.

Realising that I was wounded, they carried me off to a French casualty station, while I was deeply concerned that I was about to lose my injured leg. The French medics apologised that they had run out of anaesthetics, and that what they were about to do was likely to hurt! They gave me some morphine and then proceeded to strip my back and leg, recovering the clothing debris and splinters from my wounds – rather an unpleasant 20 minutes.

Following my 'treatment', I was placed in a schoolroom with about 12 other seriously wounded French servicemen. About every 30-60 minutes there would be a gurgling noise and one of them would die; this went on all day. I now discovered however, that the place where I had come down was called Rethel, and here by good fortune, I was found by Paul Richey. I was then loaded onto a Red Cross train for despatch to hospital in Chartres, but en route we were bombed and strafed several times.

Paul had advised Helen of my predicament and whereabouts, and she was able to bring at least some civilian clothes to me in hospital, as my service clothing had been virtually destroyed. Whilst in hospital I palled up with a French soldier who was wandering around with his steel helmet on all the time. I asked him why he did not remove it, and was told that he had been hit in the head and that half the helmet was sticking into his brain; he was still waiting for the surgeons to remove it.

Clearly there was no future for me in a French Army hospital and Helen returned to pick me up and take me to her mother's apartment in Paris. Fortunately, she was in her Spears Ambulance Corps uniform, although in her own car – a Buick – but in my civilian clothes, I obviously looked the part of a German 'fifth columnist'. As we passed through Versailles we were stopped by the police, who demanded to know why she was carrying this German blond in her vehicle.

At first they were reluctant to believe her story and wanted to put me against a wall and shoot me! It took a good 20 minutes to persuade them to get onto the British Embassy. This was no good, as the staff had already been evacuated. They then spoke to the US Embassy, who luckily knew me, due to my involvement with Helen, and were able to speak for me.

On arrival in Paris, Helen arranged for me to attend the American Hospital as an out patient while I tried to get myself sorted out and back into our own system. The US Embassy looked after me, but soon advised me to get out of Paris, as the Germans were due in the next 24 hours.

With this news, I had a drink in the Crillon Bar, then began walking back to the apartment, when I spotted a British army staff car parked outside a post office. Two British soldiers were sitting inside, and when I approached to ask what they were doing there they advised that they were waiting for a staff officer. The latter soon arrived in a little car and told me that he had been ordered to go to the Renault factory to order 1,500 light vans for the British army. I advised him of the position and suggested that he should go back to his Headquarters as quickly as possible and get the order cancelled.

When Helen realised that I had to get out of the city quick, she lent me her car, full of fuel, and I drove to Le Mans, where I had ascertained the squadron was by then based. My journey was depressing in the extreme, past lines of refugees and French soldiers with no guns, all leaving Paris. At Le Mans only the rear party remained, busy destroying unserviceable aircraft and other equipment. Once more my luck held, I was picked up by a ferry pilot and flown by him in a Fairey Battle home to England via Jersey in the Channel Islands. Back in England I made my way to Tangmere to rejoin the main body of the squadron. However, all the other chaps who I had served with for so long had been posted to operational training units to pass on the benefit of their recent experiences, so there were few around that I knew well. It hardly mattered, for I was sent on two weeks' sick leave, and then posted to Sutton Bridge for similar duties myself, where I was to join 6 OTU.

Unfortunately, this was not the same unit to which the others had gone, so for the first time since 1937 I was no longer with my 'family'.

One thing I did note as soon as I reached Tangmere was a change in attitude that had occurred so quickly that it was to stick in my brain for a long time. Here I met again the little WAAF officers who we had waved farewell to almost a year earlier. They had been so sweet and vulnerable, all enjoying their innocent love affairs with various pilots. Many of the latter were now gone for ever, and the girls involved had been badly hurt by their loss. They did not want that to happen again, and the rapid growing up this had involved had rendered them both wary and hardened. A sad but necessary early casualty of the war.

CHAPTER 4

THE BATTLE OF BRITAIN

6 Operational Training Unit, Sutton Bridge

Prior to the war, most advanced training of fighter pilots had taken place at unit level – as had been my own experience. The demands of war made this difficult to continue with, and soon after the outbreak of hostilities specialised training units had been set up to raise pilots' experience to a point where – theoretically, at least – they were ready to play their full part as soon as they joined an operational squadron.

However, June 1940 found Fighter Command reeling from the losses over France and the Dunkirk evacuation, facing imminent onslaught by the Luftwaffe, and desperate for additional pilots at the earliest possible date. Products of the Volunteer Reserve, partly trained at the outbreak of war, were now completing a foreshortened and hasty advanced training, whilst the first of the foreign pilots who had escaped from the shambles in France, were also being made ready to join British units – or soon their own national units which were to be formed under the wing of the RAF.

My job now was firstly to make certain that this mixed bag of people could actually fly, and for this purpose I first went aloft with them in Miles Master or North American Harvard advanced trainers. When satisfied that this was the case, I would send them off in Hurricanes, accompanying them in my own aircraft firstly to see if they could fly formation, and then to try and teach them the rudiments of dog fighting. Almost incredibly, with the benefit of hindsight, no provision existed for them to obtain any instruction or experience of aerial gunnery at this stage of the war.

For me this period remains in my memory as one of bloody hard work. I flew my arse off, 40-50 hours a month. During this period quite a few of my trainees where free Europeans, and I was particularly struck by some of the Poles. These great people were to a man very charming, and a lot of them were very experienced pilots, who had little to learn from me. I particularly remember Toni Glowacki who had been a corporal pilot for years in his own air force. Others who impressed me, and who went on to great things, were Stanislaw Skalski and Witold Urbanowicz, who between them became Poland's two greatest 'aces'.

Amongst the French were James Denis, who was to fly with distinction in the Western Desert, and Noel Castelain, who I believe ultimately flew with the Normandie unit on the Russian Front. Czechs too, passed through my hands, notably Frantisek Fajtl and Sgt Vaclav Cukr.

Despite living through a period of such historical significance, at the time this was not so obvious. I was still too young to have any great opinion of the wider scene. There were no briefings of what was going on – we simply read the newspapers and listened to the BBC, but knew little more than the public at large. At that stage of the war one was just too busy to visit chums at operational stations – we were just churning out the new chaps and feeding them into the system as fighter pilots as fast as we could.

But there I was, doing something that I did not really like or enjoy, and just dying to get back to a squadron on operations. My commanding officer was Wg Cdr J.H. Edwardes-Jones, and I was constantly in an out of his office, trying to achieve this. Eventually at the end of October 1940 he wangled me a posting to his old squadron 213, which at that time had recently moved to my old airfield, Tangmere. Now a Flight Lieutenant, I joined this unit at the start of October as A Flight Commander.

213 Squadron, Tangmere, and 421 Flight, Hawkinge
My new CO was Squadron Leader Duncan MacDonald, and the other flight commander was another pilot who had been in France when the 'Blitzkrieg' began – Flight Lieutenant Dennis David. I made my first flight with the squadron on 3 October and my last on the 23rd – my stay was brief. During this period I saw hostile aircraft six times, on one occasion turning in time to spot something formatting on me which turned out to be a Bf 109. I was able to claim one such probably destroyed on 10 October, whilst on the 21st, whilst leading the squadron, we were attacked by Spitfires! I also note from my logbook that every sortie I flew whilst with 21 was in Hurricane P2462.

However, after only quite a brief time with the unit, the CO called me in one day and advised that: "They are asking for volunteers for 'Jim Crow' duties – would you be interested?" At this time many of Fighter Command's radar stations had been knocked out, and whilst warning was still received of big build-ups over France, assessment of numbers, types and heights was not so easily achieved. Consequently, squadrons were having to expend much time and energy on patrols, which were not necessarily appropriate for the incoming formations.

The role of the 'Jim Crows' therefore was to fly out at very low level to shadow the incoming raiders, and to report the relevant facts relating to them, verifying and counting. The greatest danger was likely to be interception in error by one's own people. We were to be provided with a direct line to the 11 Group control room, and clearly would need to be very quick off the mark.

To undertake this new and demanding role, 421 Spotter Reconnaissance Flight was forming at Gravesend with Hurricanes, under the command of Flight Lieutenant 'Paddy' Green. Initially, we didn't know exactly what we were supposed to be doing, but two things were immediately obvious to us. Firstly, the Hurricanes with which we were initially equipped were not appropriate for the task, and secondly, if we were to avoid being attacked both by the enemy – and principally, by our own interceptors – we would need to undertake our sorties at below 10,000 feet altitude.

We got our new operations underway towards the end of the year, but already the Luftwaffe had cut back its raids to little more than fighter sweeps and occasional fighter-bomber attacks. The bombers now came mainly at night. In a word, we were redundant – we had been formed too late. We undertook patrols at our chosen levels, interspersed with fairly regular meteorological flights. In so doing, we sowed the seeds for the unit's new duties – we were to become essentially a shipping reconnaissance unit over the Channel area. In this role we would on occasion meet enemy aircraft apparently on similar duties, although fortunately for us, the Luftwaffe seemed to choose to do this with bomber aircraft, rather than fighters.

I usually flew with Sgt Gillies as my No 2 and on 6 December 1940, whilst engaged in one such patrol, we encountered a Dornier Do 17Z off the French coast, which we claimed probably shot down between us.

Before the month was out came another chance to have a go. On 27 December I was with 'Paddy' Green, when we chanced upon what we thought was a Do 215 (I now understand that this was probably another Do 17Z, the 215 being a rare beast, used only by a few reconnaissance units – but in 1940 most of us identified the later models of the Dornier in this way). Again, we claimed a probable, but I think the anti-aircraft boys saw something hit the sea, for we were subsequently advised that the Army had confirmed our success, and my logbook was annotated accordingly.

We also began flying what came to be called 'Rhubarbs' – intruder sorties into coastal areas of France by pairs of aircraft, seeking to shoot up targets of opportunity, and relying on cloud cover to escape interception. It was really a case of flat out; close eyes, and come home! Certainly, we began these operations ahead of the rest of Fighter Command, which was following suite early in the New Year.

December was also very notable for me, for on the 20th I received advice that I had been awarded the Distinguished Flying Cross. The citation read: -

"In October this officer carried out reconnaissance which proved of great value. He has at all times displayed fine qualities of leadership and perseverance. He has destroyed at least four enemy aircraft."

This was just prior to the Dornier of the 27th, the total of victories stated tying in fairly well with my own assessment of four and one shared destroyed, three and one shared probable.

On 7 January 1941 I flew four patrols, two of which brought further encounters with the foe. On the second such flight, this time with Flg Off 'Orange' O'Meara, we jointly claimed a Ju 88 damaged off Dover, whilst on the third I inflicted some damage on another of these aircraft off Folkestone – a busy day.

It was some time around this date – about two months after 421 Flight had been formed – that I received a call from the AOC, 11 Group, Air Vice-Marshal Park, who of course, knew me from his Tangmere days. I was invited to lunch, but when I arrived at Group Headquarters, Park took me straight into the Operations Room, where the great map of south-east England laid out on the plotting table, was surrounded by WAAF 'plotters', who moved round the symbols to demonstrate the position of aircraft in the air – friendly or otherwise.

At the time 421 Flight pilots were regularly 'bounced' by our own boys as much as by the Luftwaffe, and as we did not greatly appreciate such attentions, our language over the intercom was fruity on occasions, to say the least. The Ops Room was now switched to all fighter channels, and as I stood there my ears were bombarded by a stream of the most dreadful invective, which I recognised all too clearly as coming from my own pals. After listening for a few moments, Park turned to me and just said "Get the message? Now come and have lunch." Received and understood Sir!

Sadly, very shortly after this Keith Park left us, replaced by the 12 Group commander. AVM Trafford Leigh-Mallory. L-M as he was known, did not greatly care for me – I know not why. In mid January 1941, 421 Flight was expanded to become 91 Squadron, 'Paddy' Green becoming a Squadron Leader, whilst I was given command of A Flight.

I was not to remain long in my new post however – although I did experience one further event of particular note. On 2 February I went up in Spitfire 'K' on a calibration test, but when at 36,000 feet over Le Crotoy on the French coast, the engine cut out. With the amount of height in hand I was able to glide back across the Channel and force-land successfully at Hawkinge, with wheels and flaps down. Here it was discovered that a con rod had broken and burst through the side of the engine block – a lucky escape for me.

During this period however, we had, as a unit, fallen out with the airfield commander at Manston (I cannot recall why – possibly he considered us to be a scruffy and insubordinate bunch of villains!). He told Green that he did not want to see any of us on his airfield or in his Mess again. We totally ignored this, and continued to land there as and when we considered it to be appropriate and desirable to do so. This, however, seemed to give Leigh-Mallory the chance to get rid of me, and the way this was done was to "offer" me the post of Chief Flying Instructor at the OTU at Heston, commanded by Group Captain Ira Jones. I had little option but to accept, although the thought of further time off ops and on training was anathema to me.

CHAPTER 5

A NEW ERA

Training Again – 53 Operational Training Unit, Heston

As OTUs went, one could do a lot worse than 53 OTU, and I was to be in good company. Commanding Officer was that wonderful old tiger of World War I, Grp Capt Ira 'Taffy' Jones. Taffy had been a most notable fighter 'ace' in the earlier war with 74 Squadron, where he had flown with the great 'Mick' Mannock. However, despite his impressive list of victories, he lacked perception of depth in his vision, and consequently had a continuing problem when landing. He claimed to have crashed nearly as many aircraft as he had shot down, and continued in this way during the new war. Certainly he managed to break two whilst I was there, and on each occasion responded in his endearing stuttering speech; "Th-th-this aircraft is US; b-b-bring me a-a-another!" We all loved him dearly.

On a later occasion he and I had flown off in a Fox Moth to have lunch with John Cunningham. I was to fly on this occasion, but Taffy decided otherwise. "No, I-I-I'll f-f-fly, B-B-Billy-boy!" As we were preparing to take off, we were warned of a possible incoming air raid, but Taffy was not to be daunted and off we went, Taffy making a number of square turns to get us out of the circuit. There was a great clattering noise, and convinced that we were under fire from an intruder, I grabbed the controls from him and hurled the little aircraft into a series of evasive manoeuvres around some nearby trees. As I did so I happened to look down and noticed that I had not done up my seat belt, indeed one strap had got caught when the door was closed and the buckle end was flapping around outside the aircraft, beating on the fuselage whenever a sharp turn was made – with, of course, a great clattering noise. Egg on the face? Rather!!

When I first arrived at the OTU, Johnny Kent was Chief Instructor, resting after his time with the Poles of 303 Squadron and sorting out the reprobates in 92 Squadron. However, during June he went back on operations as Wing Leader at Northolt, his place being taken by that splendid man, Norman Ryder.

Two months after my arrival we moved the whole unit to Llandow in South Wales. The whole six months of my stay again proved to be hectically busy – pushing through every possible fighter pilot for the 'leaning into Europe' offensive, which was inflicting a heavy toll on Fighter Command. The demands of the other fronts – North Africa and Malta – were also increasing, whilst efforts were still being made to expand the number of fighter squadrons in the UK at a very high rate. Incredibly, the training we were giving STILL included no instruction in air firing. This still strikes me as a most extraordinary – if not almost criminal – omission in a system designed to generate effective fighter pilots.

I note from my logbook that on occasion I flew with fellow instructors – usually in a Miles Master. These included Flt Lt Roy Mottram, DFC, and Flg Off Leonard Haines, DFC. Unfortunately, the latter was killed in a flying accident shortly after my arrival with the unit. As in 1940, I chafed at being tied down to training, and constantly nagged and inveigled to get back on operations. Whether this actually reduced the time before this occurred is a moot point – but occur it did. In early September I was advised that I was to be posted out to West Africa to command a squadron there. This seemed like good news, but when I was told that my old friend, 'Killy' Kilmartin, was already there, my joy was considerable.

I made my last flight with 53 OTU on 3 September 1941; it was also to be the last flight I would make in a Spitfire for nearly two years. My logbook reminds me that at this stage of the war my own assessment of my successes to date in two years of war was five confirmed, four probable and three damaged.

A West African Adventure
It took some while to take embarkation leave, become kitted for a tropical climate, and be transported out of Freetown, Sierra Leone, aboard the SS *Nakuda* as part of a large south-bound convoy, which was on its way initially to South Africa, and thereafter to . . . well, who knows? Aboard I was made responsible for all the booze which was being carried, which amounted, I recall, to 2,500 bottles of gin and 2,000 of whiskey – a duty, which I assumed with a suitable degree of responsibility and seriousness. The ship was still manned as though in peacetime, and carried a mixture of passengers, including a number of women. So far as such a voyage can be considered a holiday cruise in wartime, it was.

On being offered a squadron, I had been glad to go and get out of training, but I really had no idea what I was about to find. I arrived therefore at the Naval airfield of Hastings to find Killy in the post of

Senior RAF Officer at the base. My 'squadron' – to be known as No 128 – had been formed from a nucleus provided from 95 Squadron, a Short Sunderland flyingboat outfit to create a local Defence Flight, with a few pilots and a skeleton ground staff, but no aircraft. That was soon settled however, four crated Hurricanes having been brought out in the same convoy in which I had travelled, and these were soon erected and being test flown. These included X4313, Z4484 and BD897. I made my first flight in the first of these on 19 October, five days after my arrival.

Our duties included guarding the convoys and units of the British Fleet, which were putting into and out of the port. Our responsibility also included the flyingboat anchorage. These were to be protected from any potential attack or other interference by the Vichy French forces based at Dakar, who had begun making reconnaissance flights over the area on occasion. As such, we were administered by Coastal Command, whose worthies had little or no appreciation or understanding of the operation of fighter aircraft; they kept asking me to do things that I really did not want to do.

Despite this, I was happy. My own promotion to wartime Squadron Leader came through at the start of December, so I was not too far behind Killy in seniority, and as his role as Senior RAF Officer at Hastings and mine as CO of 128 Squadron in no way conflicted, we were able simply to enjoy each other's company. Whilst a long way from the main focus of the war, it was nonetheless an interesting and important outpost of Empire to the observer, and I was to meet the Syrian merchant and the padre immortalised in Graham Greene's book, *So Green is my Grass*.

Force 'H', commanded by Admiral Algy Willis, victualled at Freetown, and we saw lots of sailors from here and from the convoys passing through to the Middle and Far East. I particularly remember seeing HMS *Prince of Wales* and *Repulse* as they staged through to Singapore – and recall the shock when we learned of the sinking of these mighty warships a few short weeks later. I also remember that this part of West Africa was hot – so hot that you sweated even when you were swimming. But we were young and fit, and it bothered us but little.

We were actually to see a little action over Sierra Leone, for the Vichy people could not resist coming to have a look at what was going on, even after the arrival of our fighters. They had some Glenn Martin 167F attack bombers at Dakar, which were quite fast, and were flown, I understand, by the airmen of the French Navy. One of these would occasionally stray into our airspace on a reconnaissance. On 13 December 1941 therefore – a Sunday, as I recall – I had been scrambled on the approach of one such intruder, and was patrolling over the harbour when he appeared, I flew up alongside him and indicated that he should land at our airfield, which he refused to do. This left me no alternative but to do my stuff, and shoot him down – which I did, although I did not like having to do so at all. A second of these aircraft was also to be shot down before the French in Africa rejoined the Allied cause, the successful pilot on that occasion being Sergeant Arthur Todd, who would later fly with me again in 1944, by which time he was a Flight Lieutenant on Typhoons; he subsequently received a DFC.

In January 1942 AVM Sir Keith Park passed through Freetown on his way out to take up the position of Air Officer Commanding, Egypt. When he learned of my presence, he told me: "You'll be hearing from me when I get to the Middle East." He was as good as his word for within a couple of months I received a posting to HQ, Middle East, and in March 1942 handed 128 Squadron over to my successor – Killy Kilmartin.

CHAPTER 6

TO THE WESTERN DESERT

At this time large numbers of Curtiss Kittyhawk fighters were being delivered to Takoradi, which was in the Gold Coast, not so far away from Sierra Leone – in fact 'just around the corner', so to speak. Here the Kittyhawks were being erected from crates in which they were delivered, and then being flown right across Equatorial Africa to Egypt in a series of steps. I had hoped against hope that I would be able to get a flight in an airliner or transport aircraft, but no, I was ordered to pilot one of these aircraft along that tortuous route, accompanying a group of Polish pilots. I therefore left Sierra Leone during April 1942, and without too many adventures, but decidedly weary, I reached Egypt unscathed. The worst part of the journey had been when we landed at Lake Chad, garrisoned by the Free French. It was blazingly hot, and we had to refuel our aircraft ourselves from a store of four gallon tins. The French watched, but were not about to help us.

One story did reach my ears later which was linked to these events. I asked a Provost officer some years later if we had actually put any troops against a wall and shot them during the war years, and he – to my considerable surprise – confirmed that this had indeed occurred. A number of Polish pilots had been retained to fly aircraft across the trans-African route several times. They had taken to buying industrial diamonds and getting these down to Portugal, where they were sold to German agents (Germany being desperately short of such stones) at a vast profit. Apparently they were warned by the authorities that their activities had been noted and that they should desist. They did not, were arrested and court martialled, and shot as traitors to the Allied cause.

Here I was posted to 260 Squadron as a supernumerary Squadron Leader, to learn the rudiments of the air war over the North African deserts of Egypt and Libya under the tutelage of the unit commander, Squadron Leader 'Pedro' Hanbury. At this time the unit was based on a landing ground near Gambut, just within Libya, between Bardia and Tobruk. It had fairly recently re-equipped with Kittyhawks after operating for a period with Hurricane Is, during which its losses had been far from light. I was to remain with this unit until 24 May 1942, when I would take command of 112 'Shark' Squadron. Like 260, this unit was also equipped with Kittyhawks, but had already achieved an illustrious, if not legendary, reputation in the Desert war.

I knew at once that this was going to be very different from anything I had been involved in so far. In as much as a squadron can be a 'crack' unit in the RAF, which always – officially at least – eshewed the concept of the outstanding unit – or outstanding pilot – in the interests of the team as a whole, then 112 was just such a unit. It had already enjoyed an illustrious career in the Desert and in Greece during the previous two years. Much fame had also been derived in the media, occasioned by the painting on the noses of its Curtiss fighters of a savage shark's teeth design, which had first appeared in 1941, when the initial Tomahawks had been received. When the latter were replaced by the later Kittyhawk at the start of 1942, the nose of this aircraft, with its great yawning air intake beneath the propeller spinner, was, if anything, even better suited to the paint scheme. The 'teeth' had been copied by the Flying Tigers (the American Volunteer Group) in China and Burma, and emblazoned on their Tomahawks too, and were to be painted on many other fighters as the war progressed, but I think 112 had been the first to adopt these markings at least so far as the Allied air forces were concerned. Whatever, this was how the squadron had gained its nickname.

Perhaps more importantly for me personally, was the identity of my (almost) immediate predecessor. This had been the formidable Clive 'Killer' Caldwell, a determined, personable and highly talented Australian, who had become virtually a legend during his own tour in the Desert. In less than a year Clive had claimed 19 individual and three shared victories, together with numerous others classed as probables and damaged, being awarded the DFC and Bar. His record exceeded that of any other British or Commonwealth fighter pilot in North Africa so far, by a fair margin. Quite an act for me to try and follow.

Caldwell had actually departed a few weeks before my arrival, his place initially being taken by Peter Down, who had been one of the flight commanders, but who had been taken ill shortly after assuming command. In his absence the other flight commander, Jack Bartle, another Aussie, had taken control in an acting capacity, and I am bound to say that my arrival seemed to put his nose considerably 'out of joint'. I guess he was expecting to be confirmed in the position, when suddenly this unknown 'Pom' arrived. It would have been difficult for both of us had he stayed, but within a short time he was gone, his tour having expired. The proximity of this event was probably why he had not been given the squadron, rather than any lack of suitability, as I believe he was to be given his own Kittyhawk squadron at the start of his next tour.

The pilots were a tough and experienced lot, who were unlikely to suffer gladly anyone who could not gain their confidence and inspire them. I knew at once that I was going to have to overcome a number of my existing prejudices if I was to win their acceptance. For a start, in the Desert all the pilots messed together, regardless of rank. In retrospect, this made a heck of a lot of sense, but having been brought up in the strict segregation between commissioned and non-commissioned ranks elsewhere in the RAF, at first this shocked my sensibilities. In Fighter Command the Mess had still equated to family life – one was in a sense cocooned against the rest of the world. Here it was different – and very different from 128 Squadron, which I had so recently left.

We were all still young, but it quickly dawned on me that amongst my peers were older and more experienced pilots, who were nonetheless junior to me. I was waking up to the fact that I had to become a grown man amongst men. I was an unknown quantity, and in a position of far greater real responsibility than I had ever been in before. Clearly I had to take it fairly slowly before seeking to throw my weight around, finding my feet and letting the others get to know and trust me. Fortunately, the adjutant looked after everything on the ground for me, a delegation that proved to be very necessary. This left me free to concentrate on the flying side, which was quite enough of a challenge anyway,

At our various airfields (Western Desert Air Force being a highly mobile organisation), I lived in the commanding officer's caravan, whilst the other pilots slept in tents. The Mess was a single large marquee-type tent, in which we all ate, drank and played cards together. One of my first requirements upon taking command was that all personnel shaved every morning. I insisted upon this for the purposes of morale and to enhance self-discipline – rightly or wrongly, it seemed appropriate at the time, despite the tight rationing of water.

Our diet was pretty monotonous – Spam or Machonochies – fried or whatever. There was little else. Beer was available in small quantities, and we all smoked like chimneys. The only cigarettes available were 'CtoCs', which contained South African or Rhodesian tobacco.

Everything was affected by sand – it got everywhere. Into your hair, clothing and eyes, between teeth, into your food and drink, and unfortunately, into every bit of moving machinery, where it displayed a depressingly abrasive effect. When dust storms occurred they were very unpleasant, and put an end to all civilised activity until they had abated.

Surprisingly perhaps, in these conditions, our hygiene arrangements were pretty good, and I recall little trouble from flies, which many remember as being one of the main torments they experienced in the area. That is, of course, until we took over airfields which had been occupied by the Italians. Their procedures did not seem to have been as rigorous as ours, and flies abounded.

I soon had a couple of excellent flight commanders. A Flight when I arrived, was led by a chap called Dickinson, but unfortunately he was shot down and killed shortly after I took over the unit. At much the same time Bartle departed from his place at the head of B Flight and was replaced by another Australian, Rudy Leu (known to all as 'Blue'). He was a Queenslander and a lovely chap. Absolutely reliable, "gung-ho", and really did his stuff. Within days Dickinson's place in A Flight was taken by J.A. Walker, about whom I have to admit, I recall little. Very unfortunately, neither were with us for long. Leu went down on 21 June, fortunately surviving to become a prisoner of war, whilst Walker departed again a month later to command his own squadron.

I then gained an excellent pair of flight commanders who were to remain with me for the greater part of my own tour. In B Flight Geoff Garton was posted in to replace Leu, whilst in A Flight Eric Saville, a member of the South African Air Force, joined us from one of that air force's units to fill the gap shortly afterwards. They were a pair of steady operators, both very reliable.

Amongst my other pilots, I particularly recall the Carson brothers. 'Kit' was to be shot down soon after my arrival, and just before the fighting over Bir Hacheim. This event reinforced my view that I hated having brothers in the same operational unit, as it always seemed to happen that one got killed, with a commensurate devastating effect upon the other. Happily, Kit had not been killed as we believed at the time, and was later reported to be a prisoner of war.

One of my best pilots, who arrived shortly after myself, was Desmond Ibbotson, a delightful man, sound as a rock. He could always be relied upon to do what he was told, and do it well – he was completely and utterly reliable. Of a more mercurial nature was 'Babe' Whitamore. He was a bit of an enigma; the son of an Air Marshal, I considered him to be rather a cocky little bugger. I recall one occasion when he was flying as my No 2, when we intercepted a Stuka raid, which was well-supported by Bf 109s. I was attacking one of the bombers, but broke off because I saw a stream of tracers passing beneath me. About three evenings later, when we were all having a drink, Babe admitted that he was the chap who had been firing at "the aircraft which you were failing to shoot down, Sir!" Not exactly the way to make yourself popular with your CO. I was not pleased and told him so in no uncertain terms, as I had thought that I was under fire from an enemy aircraft.

The squadron was also well-served by our Intelligence Officer, Flg Off G. Carroll. He was slightly older than most of us, and a very nice chap.

The aircraft which we flew at the time was the Curtiss Kittyhawk Mark IA – a fighter which has not always received a good 'press' since the war. My own recollections are not unfavourable. Above all, it was armed with six Browning 0.50 inch machine guns; these were superb weapons, and very reliable. They gave the aircraft, which was a very stable gun platform, a hell of a punch.

We certainly tried not to go above 10,000 feet against the Messerschmitts, as from that level downwards we could cope with them, and therefore sought to engage them at our own height. This was a rare occurrence however, as at the time I joined the squadron our role was changing. In the past the Kittyhawks, and the Tomahawks which had preceded them, had been the RAF's main air superiority and defensive fighters in the Desert. In this role they had not always found it that easy to cope with the opposition. Now Spitfires were beginning to appear to take on this function, and our AOC, 'Mary' Coningham, wanted us to change over to the ground-attack role. He had recently had it demonstrated to him that the Kittyhawk could carry a useful bomb load, and as fighter-bombers he felt we could do more to assist the army than in the past. This was a completely new role for most of us in the RAF, and we became the forerunners of the tactical ground-attack units of the Desert Air Force and of the 2nd Tactical Air Force, when the latter came to be formed.

Initially we carried a 250lb bomb beneath the fuselage, usually fitted with an extension rod to the fuse in the nose, so that it would explode just above the ground surface, allowing maximum damage to be caused to soft-skinned vehicles and personnel. So began a sharp learning curve. As we were no longer just escorting bomber formations, or undertaking sweeps or patrols over the front line, we quickly learned that navigation had become much more important in allowing us to find our targets. We also had to learn how to deliver our bombs in a medium-to-steep dive of 30-45 degrees, using the gunsight. This soon proved to be reasonably successful. We also did quite a lot of strafing with our guns.

With bombs slung beneath our aircraft and our attention focused largely on the ground, we could have been perceived as highly vulnerable to enemy attack. However, I do not recall any feeling of inferiority to the Bf 109s. Many squadron and flight commanders had flown in the Battle of Britain, and were used to Messerschmitts being about. We were also by now aware that there were not a great many of them available to the Luftwaffe in Africa.

Just at the time I took over 112, the Afrika Korps offensive against our line at Gazala commenced, just ahead of our own planned assault on their line. Immediately we were in action in our new role, and things became very busy, averaging two to four sorties a day.

My own first sortie with the squadron occurred on 26 May 1941, and did not prove auspicious. We raided Tmimi, and I recorded in my logbook: "*A good start. Brought my bomb back. What a black!*" Bombing raids were to be our main preoccupation for the next two months, leavened with the occasional fighter patrol, escort sortie or armed reconnaissance.

My first meeting with the opposition in the air occurred on 6 June. At 1015 hours that morning I led ten of our Kittyhawks on a bombing attack and reconnaissance over Bir Hacheim, where the Free French were putting up a superb resistance. Near the target we spotted four Bf 109s – below us. What luck. We dived on them and claimed the lot shot down – three confirmed and one probable, the latter being my personal contribution to events. We then bombed Axis vehicles, claiming one in flames and six damaged. Not a bad result, we felt. I note from my logbook that my notation "*Probable Me 109F*" has the word "*Probable*" struck through, and a note alongside stating "*Since confirmed by Army*". I had been flying the Kittyhawk which I had adopted as my personal aircraft, AL161, on which I had arranged that the normal individual aircraft letter was replaced with a question mark, so that it read GA-?, GA being the identification letter code allocated to the unit.

During mid June we launched several attacks on German fighter airfields around Gazala, where on the 12th I claimed one Messerschmitt destroyed on the ground, whilst on the 17th I recorded three more in flames in similar circumstances. It seems that our raids were particularly successful, for in mid July I was advised that I was receiving an immediate award of a Bar to my DFC "*for the Gazala Raid which grounded the GAF fighter force for three days.*" By the time we made these attacks however, things were not going so well on the ground, and a withdrawal from the area was beginning.

As I have indicated, my arrival with the squadron coincided with the opening of this new Axis offensive against our line at Gazala, which just forestalled our own planned attack. Rommel's Operation 'Theseus' began with an attack by the Italian infantry against the main Commonwealth lines, running south from the coast. This was designed to hold our main forces in their positions whilst his armour sought to swing south, hoping to outflank us where the defended positions petered out into the deep desert in the south, then aiming for El Adem and Sidi Rezegh.

Initially however, the southern strongpoint of Bir Hacheim, defended largely by the Free French, and with considerable support from us in the air, held firm. Fighting then concentrated in an area known to the British as 'Knightsbridge', located on the Capuzzo road between Bir Hacheim and Acroma, where the Guards Brigade had formed a defensive 'box'. Here the opposing armour clashed for several days in a battle of attrition in what became known as 'The Cauldron'.

On 4 June during one attack, I reported that I had managed to plant my bomb amongst a group of Axis troops who were apparently listening to "*a pep talk by one of their Colonels.*" It was on this date that General Ritchie, the army commander, launched a counter attack in The Cauldron, which failed to make progress. The loss of tanks by the British armoured forces at this stage was little short of catastrophic. Next day Rommel's columns over-ran the 10th Indian Brigade positions, and this proved to be the turning point of the battle in the Axis favour.

We were very active over Bir Hacheim on this date, and learned later that the French commander had sent a signal to 'Mary' Coningham, reading "*Bravo! Merci pour le RAF!*", to which Coningham had responded "*Merci pour le sport!*" By their terrific efforts, the defenders of Bir Hacheim managed to hold on until 10 June, but finally withdrew that night. They had however, prevented Rommel's armour from outflanking and encircling the troops in the main Gazala positions, who were able to undertake a reasonably orderly withdrawal.

The Afrika Korps now turned north towards El Adem and Knightsbridge, and on 14 June the Knightsbridge box was abandoned, the army heading eastwards as rapidly as it could move towards the Egyptian frontier. Tobruk was left garrisoned, ready it was thought to withstand another siege as it had done through much of 1941.

Three days later the Wing bombed and strafed the Gazala airfields, into which the Axis were once more moving, all our aircraft then withdrawing to Sidi Azeiz. Next day the airfields around Gambut which we had just departed, were in German hands, whilst on the 21st, to everyone's shock and horror, Tobruk fell.

Meanwhile on 18 June we had moved to LG 75, near Sidi Barrani, from where within two days we were bombing Sidi Azeiz. It was during these operations that we lost 'Blue' Leu, Geoff Garton arriving virtually immediately to take his place. On 28 June B Flight flew back to LG 91 at Amiriya, where it was joined next day by A Flight. We were now almost back to Alexandria, as the army – now taken over from the demoralised Ritchie, by the Middle East Supreme Commander, General Claude Auchinleck – sought to make a stand on the line which had been created at El Alamein.

This had been an extraordinary withdrawal during which we had continued throughout to provide constant air cover and support for the fleeing columns of the army below us. I am sure that what we were able to do went far in preventing that quite disastrous retreat from deteriorating into a full rout.

Certainly in 112 – and as far as I could see, in the air force as a whole – our morale remained good. Movements of this nature had been done before, and we had them off to a fine art by now. The whole of the squadron's ground echelon was divided into two parties, A and B. As the A party moved back to a new landing ground, the B party continued to service, refuel and re-arm the aircraft for as long as possible. The last to leave each airfield were the pilots and aircraft, who usually took off for an operation over the front as the B party withdrew, then landing at the new base further back, where the A party had already set up and were waiting for them. In this manner we 'leapfrogged' all the way back to Amiriya.

Of course, the situation was both worrying and confusing. There was a great deal of noise when we were on the ground, both by day and night. Often we did not know if it was our tanks or theirs which we were hearing, which could be quite traumatic at times. We relied heavily upon the intelligence services provided by HQ to let us know whether our airfield was under threat and if it was time to make a hasty departure. Every day there were vast clouds of dust everywhere as the army's vehicles rushed back and forth, collecting supplies for the troops still at the front.

Right until we got back to LG 91, we were flat out flying, bombing and strafing throughout the hours of daylight, often with our sleep disturbed at night by the events taking place all around us. We were desperately tired by the end of it, whilst for me the organisation and dangers of all the moves had brought it very much home to me that I was responsible not only for the pilots and their aircraft, but for the whole of the ground parties as well. Indeed, I had been somewhat overwhelmed by the extent to which I was personally responsible for the whole unit; thank God we had all withdrawn so rapidly and smoothly.

CHAPTER 7

STALEMATE AT EL ALAMEIN

For us by the beginning of July the retreat was at an end, but operations showed little let-up as the army fought to hold the Afrika Korps at El Alamein. On the 2nd we flew a bomber escort sortie, during which we also managed to drop a few bombs, including one of our first 500 pounders. I also managed to find and attack a Bf 109E, which was last seen going down with glycol coolant pouring from it; I was awarded a probable.

Six days later we attacked Landing Ground 21 (all landing grounds in North Africa were designated by the RAF with an LG number) as part of a Wing raid, this time dropping more 500 pounders than 250s. I also managed to bag another Bf 109. The squadron records note this as an F model, although my logbook identifies it as another of the earlier E series.

A word at this point regarding the Wing – since increasingly, now that the high-pressure panic days of May and June were behind us, we would operate as a part of this entity. We were a component of 239 Wing, which also controlled three other Kittyhawk squadrons. One of these was a fellow RAF outfit, 250 Squadron, which had been the first to receive the initial Curtiss fighters to reach North Africa, and in which Clive Caldwell had made his name before moving to command 112. The other two were both Australian units – 3 RAAF Squadron and 450 Squadron. 3 was particularly distinguished, and was home to a number of seriously tough operators. As a Wing, we had a Wing Leader, who frequently led the larger shows involving more than one squadron. At this stage the position was held by Wg Cdr Howard Mayers, who had been a Battle of Britain pilot.

However, on 20 July we took part in a Wing bombing raid on Fuka, together with 233 Wing (also comprising four squadrons flying Kittyhawks and Tomahawks – three of them South African Air Force units) and 3 SAAF Wing (a light bomber force, including squadrons flying Douglas Bostons and Martin Baltimores); it will be noted, as an aside, that the whole force was mounted on US-built aircraft. We made a thorough strafing and bombing attack, during which several aircraft were claimed destroyed on the ground by the squadron, although we lost Sgt DeBourke – who subsequently managed to make his way back to us on foot.

During this raid poor Howard Mayers, who had been seen to shoot down an Italian Macchi 202 fighter, was himself shot down, and force-landed in the wastes of the Qattara Depression. Later searching Spitfire pilots found his aircraft with the cockpit hood open, but of him there was no sign. We never heard of him again, and he was not reported as a prisoner. Many years later I learned that he was believed to have been captured, and lost when the ship carrying him to prison camp in Italy was sunk by our aircraft. What rotten luck, and what a tragic end. His place was taken by a fellow called Hislop, who proved to be a total disaster in this role. He was a nice chap personally, but just could not hack it as a Wing Leader. Very rapidly we squadron commanders agreed that we would not have him flying with us. After a very short time he was replaced by 'Billy' Burton, an ex-Cranwell regular who had been in Douglas Bader's Wing in 1940; he proved to be a very different cup of tea altogether.

July proved to be an excellent month for me. On the 23rd the squadron managed 23 sorties, dropping seventeen 500 lb bombs and four 250 pounders, although we lost two aircraft. Geoff Garton force-landed in one, but was rescued by the army and delivered back to us later that night, while Sgt Young also came down, but returned next day. I was able to claim a Macchi 202 shot down.

Next day the Wing raided LGs 20 and 104, joined by Bostons and Baltimores. We shot down three varied aircraft here, my own victim being a Bf 110, which was seen to crash and burn on the ground. I also claimed another such aircraft and a Bf 109E destroyed on the ground when we went down to strafe.

There was a wonderful story doing the rounds soon after these attacks to the effect that we had destroyed on the ground, or shot down as they were taking off, a trio of Ju 52s which proved to be in effect flying brothels, bringing comforts to the Axis troops. I had it in my mind that this had occurred on 25 July, the day after our attack on LG 20. However, I find on checking my logbook and the records of the various squadrons in the Wing, that no such claims appear to have been made on this date. It may however have happened a few days earlier when 250 and 450 Squadrons claimed three such aircraft shot down over LGs 21 and 104 on the 19th. Of course, the story regarding the contents of these aircraft may simply have been apocryphal.

However, things now quietened down considerably, and August was to prove quite a dead month after all the action of June and July. History

now tells us that Rommel and his forces could not do any more for the
moment, as they had outrun their supply lines, and these were being
seriously interdicted by the Western Desert Air Force. At sea the RAF
was also doing a good job against the shipping bringing over
reinforcements, fuel and equipment, as were the submarines and
destroyers of the Royal Navy.

This reduction in activity allowed us to let people go off to
Alexandria for the day for baths, haircuts, etc. How the barbers hated to
see us. Our dust-encrusted hair played havoc with their scissors. But a
hot bath and a good drink were what we were all really looking forward
to. Which of course, raises the question of women (or lack of them) and
arising from that, of sex. How did we keep thousands of lusty young
men on the rails for months on end with virtually no female company?
What were the repercussions of violent warfare on the natural desires
of youth? There were the usual rumours that the tea was laced with
bromide to reduce the urge, but that was probably a traditional forces
myth, which got passed on from generation to generation. In practice,
most of the time – and certainly during periods of retreat or advance –
we were much too tired (and much too disciplined) to give much
thought to the subject.

However, it was whilst we were at LG 91, one of many landing
grounds in the Amiriya area, that an event apparently occurred which
has been related by an old and dear friend of mine. Sqn Ldr Bobby
Gibbes, short of stature but great of heart, was commanding 3 RAAF
Squadron, which it will be recalled was also a part of 239 Wing. Bobby
and his wild Aussies had got wind of the fact that a number of
Australian army nursing sisters were now based at one of the military
hospitals in Alexandria. A group of these were persuaded to travel out
to Amiriya for the evening, for an impromptu party in 3 RAAF's Mess.
Of course, as the commanding officer of one of the sister squadrons, it
was only polite that I should be invited to attend.

According to Bobby, he was just "chatting up" one rather attractive
sister (or 'sheila', in Australian parlance), when I breezed over, cut him
out, and persuaded her that it would be much more fun to come over to
112's Mess and meet my pilots. Bobby says that he followed us to the
entrance to the Mess tent, and watched in disgust as I helped her into
my jeep, and prepared to drive off. He says that as I did so, I was rude
enough to turn and thumb my nose at him (would I do such an
unmannerly thing to my host and friend?), but in doing so, I drove into
a slit trench and bashed my nose on the steering wheel! If Bobby says
it happened, he must be right, for he is such a straight chap – but funnily
enough, I have absolutely no recollection of the event.

Bobby also tells me that some of his rougher Aussies considered me to be a typical stuck-up Pom officer, and were all set to sort me out. However, he apparently extolled my virtues as a fighter pilot, and forbade them absolutely from interfering with me.

One of the signs of operational tiredness that we noted was that we all tended to become overconfident as our tours progressed, and to break the rules. There was a tendency to feel that we had got to 'know it all' and to forget or ignore the basic rules – which is why, I feel, that quite a few chaps were shot down quite late in their tours. There was a distinct tendency, when landing from a successful sortie, to feel euphoric, and to want to refuel, rearm and get off again. This feeling only lasted for about half an hour, and then operational reality sobered us up.

This period therefore allowed us to sort out those who were by now in need of a rest, so that they could be relieved and sent off on non-operational duties for a while. Headquarters also decided that whole units should be given unit leaves. 112 Squadron was one of those so favoured, and we all departed to Beirut in the Lebanon for a few days relaxation. Another story arose at this time. We were advised that the Luftwaffe magazine, *Signal*, reported during this period that their great fighter ace, Marseille, claimed to have shot down the leader of the Shark's Mouth Kittyhawks twice during this period, at a time when we were not even in Egypt. Once again, with the benefits of access to records that were not available to us in those days, I have been shown to my satisfaction that Marseille made no claims between mid June and the end of August 1942, so this must have been a real bit of propaganda 'hype'.

There were also some significant changes in overall command at this time. Auchinleck, who had taken over direct control of the army from General Ritchie during the Gazala debacle, was sent off to India, his place being taken as Commander-in-Chief by Sir Harold Alexander, while Eighth Army – as the North African army now became – received Bernard Montgomery as their new direct commander. Intelligence was well aware that Rommel was stalled until he could be resupplied, and the new team began preparations for the next phase.

CHAPTER 8

ALEM EL HALFA AND ALAMEIN

At the end of August Rommel launched his next offensive, designed to break through our line at El Alamein and finally reach Alexandria, Cairo and the Suez Canal Zone. This time he attacked at the south end of the line, hoping undoubtedly to repeat his outflanking success at Gazala. However, here the situation was to prove different in two important respects. Unlike the Gazala position, where our line effectively petered out into open desert at the end of its left flank, here it was anchored on the almost impassable salt flats of the Qattara Depression.

Further, our new commander, Montgomery, was well aware of his likely intentions, and by cleverly preparing extremely strong defensive positions in the strictest secrecy, had 'suckered' his opponent into entering a trap. Several days of intensive fighting, during which we in the air force launched a maximum effort against the Axis columns, were followed by a rather ignominious retreat, as Rommel realised that the Eighth Army was too strong here, and that he had bitten off more than he could chew.

It was 112's good fortune to run into a formation of Ju 87 Stukas on 1 September during a sweep over the Qat el Abd area. We were able to claim four of them shot down; two of these were credited to me, raising my confirmed total to a round dozen.

As the German attack melted away, a period of relative calm again descended on the ground battle, as the Commonwealth forces steadily built up their supplies for our own forthcoming offensive. The presence of our American allies in the war – now nine months since Pearl Harbor – began to become more obvious at this time. Large numbers of the new Sherman heavy tanks were appearing to supplement the Crusaders, Valentines and existing US-built Stuarts (Honeys) and Grants. We were later to learn that President Roosevelt had again interceded to the British advantage, directing that the first available production Shermans should go to our forces rather then those of his own country.

More immediately visible to us however, where the first units of the US Army Air Force, as Martin B-25 Mitchell medium bombers joined our Bostons and Baltimores, and P-40F Warhawks of the 57th Fighter Group arrived to join us. The P-40F was basically similar to our Kittyhawk, but had been re-engined with a version of the Rolls-Royce Merlin, built under licence by Packard in the States. We were later to get a few in the Wing for our own use, where we knew them as the Kittyhawk Mark IIa. Perhaps because of the improvements in the altitude performance that the Merlin appeared to promise, many British pilots referred to them as "Goshhawks"!

We quickly found that the US pilots were superbly trained and very experienced in flying their aircraft. Virtually to a man they were peacetime professionals, similar to Fighter Command's boys back in September 1939, and many of them were West Pointers. However, they had no operational experience at all of course, although they were generally very keen to learn from us.

To facilitate their learning, Mary Coningham suggested attaching me to their Group to act as Wing Leader, but US rules did not permit this. Instead, one of their squadrons was attached to 239 Wing and 112 Squadron took its place in the 57th. Effectively, this allowed me to lead them for a few weeks until it became quite obvious that they had picked up what was needed. They were a great bunch, and I think they respected us. Certainly the feeling was mutual.

I have alluded above to the improvement which it was perceived a new engine might bring to our aircraft. The early versions of the Allison which powered the Kittyhawk I suffered from desert conditions as the bearings appeared to be too soft, and were worn away rapidly by the abrasive effects of the sand. We realised subsequently that the Egyptian contractors who were servicing our engines in the Cairo area, were not taking enough care in keeping sand out, and this exacerbated the problem. In the event the arrival of new, better, phosphor-bronze filters helped to improve the situation.

During the period from mid September to late October, we were kept very busy, attacking the Axis airfields – particularly those where their fighters were based – undertaking sweeps and bomber escorts, and on occasion becoming involved in interception patrols, as the Luftwaffe tried to bomb our lines. On one such occasion during the evening of 13 September I was able to claim one Bf 109F probably destroyed and a second damaged, but to my good fortune the army again confirmed that they had seen the former of these crash. Another interception on the first day of October – again in the evening – once more allowed us to get amongst the Stukas, almost exactly a month since our previous meeting with them. We considered that we had again administered a good hiding to these dive bombers, this time claiming three confirmed and two probables. I was able to claim one of those shot down, share a second with Geoff Garton, and also claim one of the probables – personally a highly satisfying result.

On a sweep over the Axis airfields in the Daba area on the 22nd, I claimed another Bf 109F as a probable, and for me that brought the 'quiet' period to an end. Soon after darkness had fallen next evening, the huge artillery barrage that heralded the opening of the Alamein offensive, impressed and excited us all. The next few days, as the battle raged in all its fury, we were out daily either escorting the mediums to attack the Axis concentrations and their supply areas immediately behind the front, or making our own bombing and strafing attacks on these same targets. During October, ready for the new offensive, we had been re-equipped with the new Kittyhawk III – again with an Allison engine, but with a number of improvements in detail, including a somewhat extended tail fin. Although the uprated engine offered us an additional 175 horse power, the effect on performance was negligible – and indeed, we had by now learned that for all its Merlin engine, the Mark II also performed almost exactly like the Allison versions.

The activities in which we were now involved soon proved productive and profitable for the squadron, and for me personally, both in the destruction we wrought on the ground, and in terms of enemy aircraft shot down. I was able to claim an Italian Macchi 202 fighter over the northern sector of the line on 26 October (once again conveniently confirmed for me by the army), and a second of these next day when escorting bombers to attack LG 18 at Fuka.

On the 30th we provided cover to the US 66th Fighter Squadron (part of the 57th Group), strafing LG 21, where I was able to claim an He 111 and a Bf 109 in flames on the ground, with a second Messerschmitt damaged. The last day of the month filled my cup to overflowing when, whilst bombing targets in the northern sector again, we once more encountered Stukas, and I was able to add two more to my personal tally.

At the start of November, after days of hammering, the Axis forces at last began to break, and as the month progressed a withdrawal – which quickly came to resemble a rout – became visible. For us it was a hectic month, but again a profitable one. It was clear that apart from the growing confusion that they were suffering on the ground, the Axis were also short of petrol. We caught more of their aircraft on the ground, suffered less from attacks by their fighters, and started meeting transport aircraft as these attempted to fly forward loads of fuel and other urgent supplies.

During a strafing attack on LG 21 at Gazala on 2 November, I was able to set fire to a pair of tri-motor Ju 52s and a Bf 109. Next day over Fuka once more, I claimed a Bf 109F destroyed and a second damaged. We caught Messerschmitts with their engines running at Gambut on the 12th, and I was able to claim two of these destroyed and a third probably so before they could take off. On 14 November during an armed reconnaissance over the Cirene area, I encountered an He 111 bomber – probably pressed into use as an emergency transport – and was able to send this down to crash.

Finally on the 19th we were scrambled during the afternoon to intercept intruders, meeting Bf 110s – the first I had seen in a long time. I claimed one of them shot down and one damaged. A few days later on the 26th I received the news that the King had graciously awarded me the Distinguished Service Order.

By now however, I was getting close to the end of my tour, but I was determined not to go yet if I could avoid it. The main reason for this was because the squadron was fast approaching its 200th confirmed victory, and I hoped to be there to help celebrate that momentous event. I managed to stay until mid January 1943 in practice, but the reduction in opposition in the air coupled with the increasing focus of our operations towards ground-attack work, was reaching a level where opportunities for claiming were becoming much rarer. The magic figure was not to be reached whilst I was there, sadly.

Less was happening in early December, and I note from my logbook that I flew a captured Ju 87 for 25 minutes on 4th, and got half an hour in a Spitfire four days later. We were out with the US 66th on both 10 and 11 December, bombing targets on the ground – notably German panzers on the latter date – when an event occurred that almost brought a rather violent conclusion to my career as a fighter pilot and squadron commander. We became heavily involved with a considerably more than average-sized force of enemy fighters, and during this I was attacked by seven Bf 109Fs, although I was able to avoid them successfully by diving into cloud at 6,000 feet. When I emerged to pinpoint my position however, I was again attacked and had to take more evasive action. During these actions I was able to claim both a Messerschmitt and a Macchi shot down, but now I ran out of fuel and was obliged to put my poor Kittyhawk (FR293) down on its belly amongst the forward reconnaissance troops – men of the 11th Hussars armoured car regiment ('The Cherrypickers') – who rescued me and helped me to get back to the squadron.

My final action in North Africa occurred during a bombing attack south of Agheila on 13 December, when I was able to share another Bf 109F shot down with Sgt Shaw. Thereafter, whilst I undertook the odd patrol, most flights were concerned with moving from airfield to airfield as we pursued the Afrika Korps towards southern Tunisia. On 16 January 1943 my posting at last came through, and I was off to Headquarters, Middle East, to join 203 Training Group for the next six months.

During the time that I led 112 Squadron – probably the most eventful, exciting and formative period of the war for me – I had increased my own successes against enemy aircraft to 23½ destroyed, nine probables and six damaged, plus a number shot up on the ground. I note that I recorded the latter as comprising three when making up the page at the end of December 1942, but this had been revised to 13 some months later. Although I had by then added a few more in this category, on looking back through the book, the earlier total does indeed appear to have been a considerable underestimate of what I had actually claimed.

So what had been achieved during my first 'real' command? I like to think that the results had been worthwhile. We had done a vast amount of ground-attack work in support of the army. This had seemed to be effective, but is notoriously difficult to measure with any degree of precision. Undoubtedly, the two Kittyhawk wings had also provided extremely effective escort to the light bomber wings, whose casualties to Axis fighters had been negligible whilst under our care.

It is perhaps somewhat easier to assess what we had done in action against our opposite numbers in the Luftwaffe and Regia Aeronautica – always allowing for the element of over-claiming which we now know tends to occur in all such situations. When I arrived on the squadron, the 137th claim for a hostile aircraft had just been made. When I departed some eight months later, claims had reached 199 (on 13 January 1943). Thus during that period some 62 German and Italian aircraft had been claimed shot down – quite a few of them Messerschmitt Bf 109Fs, which were superior to our Kittyhawks in several of the key aspects of performance. We had also claimed 28 probables and 33½ damaged, together with a fair number of aircraft destroyed on the ground.

During that same period, apart from myself, some 70 or so pilots had served with the unit. Of these, between late May 1942 and the end of January 1943, 15 had been killed or were listed as 'Missing', while ten more were prisoners of war (so we had lost more than a third of those who had flown with us). Of course, quite a number of other aircraft had been brought down where the pilots had survived unhurt (myself on at least one such occasion). In total we lost 55 Kittyhawks to enemy action of one sort or another – fighters and flak – but nonetheless, I like to think that we came out of it all somewhat better than even. And let's not beat about the bush – at that time the opposition was good – bloody good!

In the air, the 17 and two shared aircraft shot down, plus two probables, that had been credited to me since joining 112 in May 1942, had been exceeded as a total in North Africa only by Clive Caldwell, my predecessor as squadron commander. I am bound to add however, that we were both subsequently to be overtaken by Neville Duke (himself an ex-member of 112 Squadron) and by the American-born Lance Wade – but not until some time later.

Some Comments on Aerial Combat

Since the war years I find that I have frequently been asked what it was like to be involved in aerial combat or dogfighting. I have always found it difficult to commit to paper my true memories of these engagements, other than to state that I usually experienced a mixture of wild excitement as I worked out how to get within firing range of my opponent as quickly as possible. Coupled with this was the hope that my No 2 was watching my tail, the nasty thought always being there that somewhere in the airspace a complete stranger was seriously intending to kill me should I be stupid or careless enough to give him half a chance.

To these factors must be added the fact that flying an aircraft is a three-dimensional task, and is therefore an additional, but vitally important element when seeking to discuss air combat. Further, aircraft tend to have limited endurance, and therefore time for all concerned was usually also a limiting consideration. The net result of these factors was that typical air combat situations were of very short duration (not lasting more than minutes at the most), and included target identification, decisions regarding tactics to be employed, and actual execution. A leader also had to assess the overall situation and allocate targets or tasks to the various sub units and pilots. Speed of thought, quick reactions and the ability to assess situations rapidly were the essential requirements of successful leadership in controlling and leading fighting units, which might be anything from four aircraft to wings of two squadrons (24 aircraft). A natural gift of leadership together with combat experience were the qualities looked for and required at every level from flight commanders to squadron and wing leaders. During World War II these qualities were usually to be found in the young, and the average age of my contemporaries tended to be around the mid 20s.

On the other hand, it is interesting to note that the US Air Force contradicted this statement later in that WW II veterans frequently proved to be the outstanding aces and leaders in Korea and Vietnam. This can be put down to the vast and relevant combat experience they had obtained in the earlier war, and the continuation and development of their natural leadership qualities.

My recollections of actual combat sorties are still vivid, but unfortunately the time factor related to each such episode was of such short duration that even at debriefings immediately after the event, my recollections of what had happened only some 40 minutes earlier were beginning to fade and were sometimes at variance with what *had* actually happened.

This, of course, differed between individuals, but it must be remembered that air combat included a large element of ensuring survival, and most of us were glad to be alive. The reaction which followed differed from person to person; some were inclined to embellish their experiences, but most were grateful that the episode was over and that a mug of tea would go down well as soon as the debriefing was completed.

From the above it will be appreciated that when I seek to discuss my memories of specific air combats and attempt to draw a picture of typical events, I find that I suffer from a memory block. All I can see is a collection of confused events, culminating sometimes in a victory, sometimes in a series of wild evasive actions caused by enemy counter-actions. As I have said, aerial fighting usually takes place in seconds rather than even in minutes, making it very difficult now to recall any particular action. Even at the time it was usually only possible to assess the outcome of a particular engagement once the enemy had left the airspace involved, and one could count one's losses and/or victories.

Some pilots are blessed with photographic memories; some, like Paul Richey, kept detailed diaries (strictly contrary to orders then in force!) to augment their brain cells. Most of us however, had no intention at the time to write autobiographies, and therefore allowed our memories to lie dormant. Furthermore, the time lapse between the 1940s and today represents some 60 years, and therefore one must be forgiven if the memories of specific events have dulled with time, or have been affected by what one has read or been told of since.

CHAPTER 9

TRAINING AGAIN

203 Group, which I now joined, was responsible for the operational training of all units in the Middle East. Soon after my arrival I was sent for a month's liaison with 335 Squadron – the first fighter unit in the RAF formed with Greek personnel. My role was to introduce them to RAF operations, and particularly to ground attack. They flew Hurricanes, an aircraft with which I was, of course, very closely familiar.

Following this interesting posting, I was detailed to go down to Kenya to close up two Blenheim OTUs at Nakuru and Nanyuki. The Blenheim was by now considerably obsolescent as a bomber and was rapidly being replaced in front line units by more modern types. Thus the call for replacement crews was rapidly declining. This promised to be something of a 'jolly', and I flew down to Nairobi in a Sabena (Belgian airline) aircraft, and thence by Imperial Airways Empire flyingboats to Léopoldville and Stanley Falls. Amongst the other passengers was General Anders, the Polish commander of their forces in the Middle East.

I spent about a month in Kenya, sorting things out, and during this time was converted onto the Blenheim myself. Meanwhile during March I was also promoted Acting Wing Commander. With the OTUs closed, I intended to fly a Blenheim back up to Cairo, to where all the remaining airworthy examples of such aircraft were to be delivered. I planned to lead a formation of these aircraft, piloted by the various instructors and senior pupils. The flight would need to be undertaken in several stages, and would involve a total of about 21 hours in the air.

On the appointed day I introduced myself to the navigator who was to accompany me, and having started the engines, took off in a fighter manner, expecting the rest to follow me. To my surprise and annoyance, this they failed to do, and I never saw any of them again throughout the journey. Worse was to come, for when I turned to the navigator and asked for a course, he hadn't a clue. It turned out that he had got into the wrong aircraft. I therefore asked him to pass me his maps and help us to reach Victoria Falls. From there I simply followed the Nile up to our destination. We landed at Cairo very much alone about three days later.

The rest of my time with the Group was spent in a hotel in Heliopolis, with what was very much a desk job, generally training staff. My happiest memory of this period was of getting to know Stan Grant, a fellow Wing Commander, who had survived two tours on Malta during the height of the 'Blitz' on that island. I recall that we got pissed together a few times.

With such a variety of duties, my time off operations passed quite rapidly, and on 14 June 1943 I was posted to Malta to join Keith Park's Headquarters there. The very day that I arrived, John Ellis, who was leading the island's Krendi Wing, was shot down over Sicily and taken prisoner. Park at once told me to take over his place as Wing Leader – and I was back on Spitfires again. Obviously, after my time with 112 Squadron I had expected to be selected for a ground-attack role, anticipating perhaps leading a wing of Kittyhawks – but a return to the primary air fighting function was not a matter which depressed or dismayed me, particularly as each of my squadrons had four Spitfire IXs to supplement their Mark Vs.

The units of the Wing were all veterans of the long defensive battles, and were possessed of impressive credentials; they were numbered 185, 229 and 249 (the latter incidentally, would end the war as the RAF's highest-scoring fighter unit).

My arrival coincided also with the build-up for the forthcoming invasion of Sicily. Units from North Africa were being transferred to Malta at a great rate of knots, and the congestion in the air above the island was becoming absolutely chaotic. The air controllers had quite a job simply keeping it all under control, let alone directing the various operations being undertaken towards Sicily.

By this time the whole of North Africa had fallen to the Allies, and air superiority over the Axis had reached a pretty advanced stage. We were involved in the main in undertaking offensive fighter sweeps over Sicily in an effort to bring our German and Italian opposite numbers into action. We also escorted a wide variety of bomber types over that island, including growing numbers of four-engined B-17 Flying Fortresses and B-24 Liberators.

On 21 June we swept over Comiso airfield, then going down to strafe, and once more I was able to claim a couple of Messerschmitts destroyed on the ground here. We saw a few fighters in the air on the 28th and 29th, and while I was able to get a quick shot at a Macchi on the first such date, I could not achieve any conclusions, although next day some of my pilots did manage to get a couple of confirmed and some damaged.

My chance at last came on 7 July when we covered B-17s to Gerbini, where I shot down an MC 202. I have subsequently discovered that by a strange coincidence, this aircraft was from the same unit as that which I had shot down on 17 October 1942 over Africa – the 97ªSquadriglia of the 9°Gruppo CT, from the Regia Aeronautica's 4°Stormo.

On 10 July 1943 the British 8th and US 7th Armies invaded Sicily from an armada of 2,500 vessels supported by a substantial paratroop and glider drop. For us, the whole invasion proved a rather dull affair, as the Axis air forces were by then more obvious by their absence than by their actions. Throughout that huge affair, only six ships were to be sunk.

One of the disadvantages of being a Wing Leader I was finding, was that invariably I had to fly the slowest aircraft – usually therefore a Mark V. The Spit IX was a wonderful aircraft, and boasted a two-stage supercharger which came in automatically at 18,000 feet, with an impressive surge of power. When I first took one up, I had not been warned about this, and as I was climbing up to reach operational altitude of about 30,000 feet, quietly minding my own business, there was suddenly an almighty bang as the supercharger came in and I was almost knocked through the back of my seat. Subsequently we cut out the automatic control and operated the thing manually so that we could prepare ourselves for the explosion of power when we wanted to.

The commanding officers of my three units were all good guys – highly experienced and competent. 249 had been led for some time by an ex-Eagle Squadron American, J.J. Lynch, but soon after I joined the Wing he was replaced by 'Timber' Woods. 185 Squadron was commanded by Neil MacDougall, DFC, like myself an ex-Kittyhawk pilot who had previously led a flight in 260 Squadron in the Desert. 229's 'boss' was Blair White, but he was lost quite early on, and his place was taken by Graham Cox. When leading the Wing I usually flew with 249 Squadron.

As the fighting in Sicily moved to the north side of the island, most of the units which had been brought over from North Africa now departed Malta for airfields which had been captured along the southern Sicilian coastal belt. Consequently, as one of Malta's resident units, we reverted to the air defence role after 19 July, in which there was now really very little for us to do.

After this had gone on for a month with little but air tests and practices to keep us occupied, Timber Woods and I worked out a rather more entertaining little adventure. On 20 August we flew our Spitfires over to a disused airfield on the eastern side of Sicily, known as Termini. Having refuelled, we took off again and proceeded up the Italian coast at very low level to have a look at Naples.

As we flew, the sea was dead calm and it became somewhat difficult to judge the height at which we were flying. Timber was a little way behind me, and I radioed him "Move up and give us some ripples!", and he came alongside me, so that I could see the effects of his propeller wash on the surface of the water, and he could do likewise by looking across at mine. As it turned out, there was not a lot to be seen, and having strafed anything which appeared to be worth strafing, we cleared off again in a hurry, landing back at Termini after three hours and ten minutes in the air. Our caution in making the outward flight at so low a level where we could not be picked up by radar seems to have paid off, for no attempt to intercept us was made.

By this time I was again very tired, and at the start of October I completed this relatively short tour, and prepared to return to the United Kingdom. My journey home proved interesting, for I sailed aboard the battleship HMS *Rodney*. This was an excellent opportunity to see how the navy operated – having seen much of the army's way of doing things whilst in the Desert. It certainly appeared to me to be a most gentlemanly way of going to war –they even dressed properly for dinner each evening! I shared a cabin with the Chief Torpedo Officer, and was appointed Chief Spotting Officer for enemy aircraft for the duration of the voyage. In practice I was only twice asked to go up to the 'Crow's Nest' to undertake this function, the first time being as we departed Malta. As I perched on high, an aircraft passed nearby, towing a drogue sleeve target, and at this the whole Fleet opened fire. I had not been warned of this forthcoming practice, and had been given no advice as to my personal safety in such circumstances! As tracers floated past me, at times quite alarmingly close by, I had no idea whether the 'Crow's Nest' was protected, or was in danger of being peppered by its own side.

Nevertheless, I survived unhurt, if somewhat mortified, and enjoyed the rest of the trip, reaching England, Home and Beauty on 12 November following an absence of some two years. On arrival I was granted three weeks leave, and then posted as Wing Commander Flying – 'Wing Leader' – of 20 Wing at 136 Airfield. This unfamiliar nomenclature was all to do with the new 2nd Tactical Air Force, which had recently come into being, ready for the forthcoming invasion of Western Europe. 20 Wing was controlled by the new 84 Group, although for the time being all operational direction remained in the hands of good old 11 Group. 136 Airfield was Fairlop, a satellite landing ground in the North Weald Sector. Its units were 164 and 195 Squadrons, flying an aircraft which was new to me – the Hawker Typhoon Ib.

CHAPTER 10

WITH THE SECOND TACTICAL AIR FORCE

The commanding officer of the Wing was Grp Capt C.E. St. J. Beamish, DFC, but he was effectively a purely administrative commander, and never flew whilst I was there – that was very much my preserve. But what a massive great aircraft the Typhoon was. Nearly twice as powerful as anything I had flown before, and very fast – over 400 mph at quite low level, and fairly rugged. At the time I arrived most of the 'bugs' had been ironed out of it (for it had been possessed of plenty earlier in its career), but it still had one persistent and unfortunate fault. The driving spindle from the engine to the fuel and oil pumps was not robust enough and tended to shear, leaving one with an embarassing lack of engine – and the Typhoon was most <u>definitely</u> not an aircraft to ditch in the sea, with its massive oil cooler intake under the nose. Indeed, it was not too promising to crash-land either, and required great care and good luck not to dig in that intake and flip over onto its back. Coupled with the low altitudes at which we usually operated, there was not much chance of baling out, so one could be between the Devil and the deep blue sea – quite literally. Fortunately, the problem was diagnosed, and before long all engines were modified to incoporate an upgraded spindle.

On the plus side the four 20mm cannons provided a most formidable armament, and the aircraft could carry an impressive load of bombs or rocket projectiles (RPs).

So here I was, back into a tactical air force type of environment, and happy to be there. Due to my Desert experience I was, of course, fully used to such operations and felt that my skills and talents were now to be put to best use as an invasion of France was felt by all to be on the cards sooner rather than later, and only a matter of time.

Our initial targets were to a large extent what were known as 'No-balls'. These were launching sites that were being constructed in growing numbers in the Pas de Calais – at the time for reasons that were far from clear to us. Of course, all too soon we would become aware that they were for launching the V-1 flying bombs against south-east England.

These sites were generally located quite close to the coast, and increasingly were heavily defended by flak. To avoid early radar identification, we tended to fly over the Channel at zero feet, climb rapidly to 6,000 feet on reaching the coast, slip into line abreast or line astern formation, and dive on the target, dropping bombs or firing rockets, and strafing. Doing this with 12, or even 24 aircraft required very precise navigation by the leader, since it was vital to cross the coast at exactly the right place if surprise was to be maintained, make the attack and be gone. You were not going to go round a second time on THAT scenario.

Whilst at Fairlop I was on one occasion given a 'No-ball' site to attack with 24 aircraft, each carrying two 500lb bombs. As was normal operational procedure, that entailed flying as low as possible over the outskirts of London and out across south-east England. As I approached Bromley in Kent, my engine spluttered once and then cut out completely. I instructed my deputy leader to take over, and pulled up to assess what my prospects for a force-landing were. To my surprise and delight, I then saw Biggin Hill below me and at once informed the control tower there of my predicament and my intention to force-land there at once. As I had been cruising at about 350 mph, I had plenty of time to gain height and position for such a task. As a Spitfire Wing was taking off at that moment, I was told to land on the short north-south scramble runway so as not to abort the Spits. As there was little or no wind, I had decided to land with my wheels up; this meant that I would actually be landing on the two 500lb bombs which were attached to the undersides of my wings. This in turn posed a problem because I had considered on setting off, the wisdom of switching my bombs to 'armed' after take-off, so that I would eliminate one thing to remember when over the target area. I realised that I could not now remember what my decision had been in this respect on this particular mission. As I was now fully occupied with trying successfully to force-land a grossly overloaded Typhoon, I had no time to look at the position of the arming switches, which in any case were quite difficult to see at the best of times.

To cut a long story short, I was in luck as the bombs were on 'safe', so no harm was done. As we wing leaders were to be briefed by General Eisenhower that afternoon, I was in my best No.1 uniform and had already taken off my flying kit when the Medical Officer and an ambulance arrived, and was somewhat surprised to be asked if I knew were the pilot was!!

During my initial period with the Wing I attended the Specialised Low Attack Instructors School (SLAIS) at Milfield, where all squadron and wing leaders were being sent to be shown how effective bombs and

Myself as a Wing Commander during the 1950s.

Top: Around the time I departed for school in Switzerland, my parents moved from Stroud and built this house - named Ashe House, after the family home in Devon - at Wigmore, near Chatham, Kent. The young lad on the front lawn with the dogs is indeed myself; this was the holiday when I collected my boxing gloves to defend England's honour!

Bottom: Gerald Coulson sketched this 1 Squadron Hawker Fury for me in a matter of minutes. It is also signed by my old friend, 'Paddy' Barthropp.

Top left: Always the keen skier, here I am on the piste at Megevre during my last day of such sport in 1939, prior to the outbreak of war.

Top right: Myself, immediately after claiming my first successes in April 1940.

Bottom: Some of Fighter Command's very first Hawker Hurricane Is lined up for the photographer. This was 111 Squadron, the first unit to receive the aircraft a little before us, and was almost certainly at Northolt. In the right background are some of the Fairey Battles which we fighter boys used to transition onto this modern monoplane. In the left background is a Hawker biplane, probably of the Hart family. Hurricane L1550, clearly visible here, had a short life, being destroyed in a forced landing at Colnbrook in July 1938.

\ well-known, but wonderful shot of much of 1
on's officer strength in France early in the war.
ight are: myself, Leslie Clisby, Lorrimer, Prosser
3oy' Mould, 'Bull' Halahan (CO), Jean 'Moses'
(interpreter), 'Johnnie' Walker, the Medical
ıl Richey, 'Killy' Kilmartin, Bill Stratton and
ner. Probably the most notable pilot missing

from this group is our Canadian, 'Hilly' Brown.
Bottom left: My greatest pal, 'Killy' Kilmartin.
Bottom right: Getting into my 128 Squadron
Hurricane.

Top: A Curtiss Kittyhawk Ia of 112 Squadron at the time that I took command of the unit. Note the 250lb bomb beneath the fuselage, fitted with an extension rod to the nose fuse. Plt Off Henry Burney, RAAF*, was lost in this aircraft, AK772 (named 'London Pride') a few days after my arrival.

Middle: With a member of the ground crew sitting on the wingtip to help the pilot find the take-off point, shrouded in dust and obscured by the engine nascelle, a 112 Squadron Kittyhawk taxies out for a fighter-bombing sortie.

Bottom right: With my Hurricane of 128 Squadron at Hastings, Sierra Leone, around the time I shot down the Vichy French Glenn Martin 167 'snooper'.

Top: This was one of the Kittyhawks which I flew, ET790. In this aircraft I claimed a Messerschmitt Bf 109F shot down on 8 July 1942. Before the month was out, this aircraft too had failed to return, Plt Off J.S.Barrow being lost to flak whilst flying it. Note that on this occasion the bombload has been doubled, and it is carrying a 500 pounder.

Middle left: Armourers fixing a 250lb bomb in place under the belly of one of our Kittyhawks during summer 1942.

Middle right: Grp Capt Guy Carter, SASO, Western Desert Air Force, in a Hurricane. Guy was to be killed accidentally when being flown into Yugoslavia in a Dakota later in the war.

Bottom: Very much the veteran fighter pilot by 1942, here I am enjoying one of the cigarettes without which we were rarely to be seen by this time. The scarf was one of those specially produced each year for the Derby winner, this one having been in respect of a horse called Hyperion. It had been given to me by the lady owner (whose name sadly I no longer recall) whilst I was serving in France in 1940. I used it throughout the war.

Top: 'Top Brass' in the Desert. Left to right: Grp Capt Guy Carter, Air Marshal 'Mary' Coningham, Grp Capt Fred Rosier and Wg Cdr T.B. de la Poer Beresford** (in solar topee). Sitting in the doorway of the command vehicle is Wg Cdr Howard Mayers, and at extreme right, in dark glasses, is Grp Capt Harold Fenton**.

Bottom: Here I am seen with three of my pilots when commanding 112 Squadron. I cannot recall the names of the two on the left, but the young man on the right is 'Babe' Whitamore, a promising fighter pilot who was later lost in Burma.

Above: No 1 Course at the Fighter Leaders' School, Milfield, in early 1944. The galaxy of talent here includes many notable fighter pilots and leaders. Our first CO, Grp Capt Adams (front row, 6th from left) is flanked my myself (still with the fag in my mouth and my 'Hyperion' scarf, it may be noted), and by newly-promoted Grp Capt Jamie Rankin. Others who have been identified include: Front row: Wg Cdr Johnny Baldwin* (3rd from left), Wg Cdr 'Johnnie' Walker (8th), Reg Grant* (9th), Stanislaw Skalski (10th), Tom Balmforth** (1

Bottom: My A Flight commander, Eric Saville, SAAF (left), considers the damage suffered by his Tomahawk whilst serving with 2 SAAF Squadron, shortly before he joined 112. He is accompanied by a war correspondent with whom he is discussing his lucky escape.

Pete Wickham (12th) and Eric Thomas*. Second row: Cdr Sinclair-Forbes (4th from left), Wg Cdr B. Ingham** (5th), Maj Frasier (6th), 'Dizzie' Allen* (7th), Keith Lofts* (8th), Wg Cdr Brown, GCI controller, (9th), and Col Kaj Birksted* (11th). Third row: Mike Donnet** (4th from left). Fourth row: Gordon Sinclair* (3rd from left), George Keefer*, (6th). Rear row: Erik Haabjoern** (4th from left), Humphrey Russel (11th).

Bottom: Preparing for the September 1945 Battle of Britain Day Anniversary Flypast: left to right, myself (barely in the picture), Grp Capt Frank Carey (adjusting his watch), Grp Capt J.M.Thompson*, Wg Cdr Bob Stanford Tuck, Wg Cdr John Ellis, Wg Cdr Tim Vigors*, Wg Cdr Denis Crowley-Milling*, Grp Capt Douglas Bader (back to camera), Wg Cdr Keith Lofts*, ACM Lord Dowding, Wg Cdr 'Hawkeye' Wells* (back to camera), and (hidden) Wg Cdr Peter Brothers and Sqn Ldr Roy Bush*.

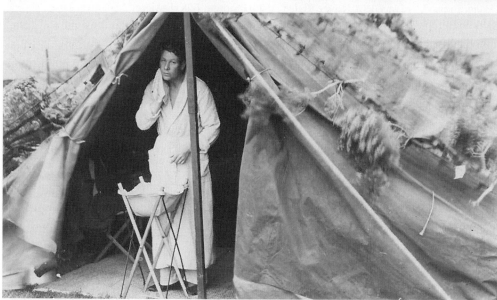

Top left: My tour with 112 Squadron at an end, I was sent back to Egypt on administrative duties. Here I was presented with the US DFC by General Brereton, this medal hanging beneath the ribbons of my DSO, DFC and Bar immediately after the ceremony.

Top right: My good friend, Bobby Gibbes, RAAF, commanding officer of 3 RAAF Squadron in our 239 Wing.

Bottom: Back in England it was still rough living as we prepared for life in continental Europe after the invasion. Here I undertake my ablutions at 20 Sector's airfield, Thorney Island, on the Hampshire coast.

Top: Spitfires prepare for the Battle of Britain Day Anniversary Flypast, September 1945. Douglas Bader is in the foreground in DB- 'Dogsbody' (his 1941 callsign).

Bottom: The Flypast over London, 15 September 1945. The 'spike' in the foreground is thought to be a captured German V-2 rocket.

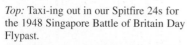

Top: Taxi-ing out in our Spitfire 24s for the 1948 Singapore Battle of Britain Day Flypast.

Bottom left: I ski at St Moritz in 1949/50 as part of the RAF Team.

Bottom right: With an Airspeed Oxford at CFE, West Raynham, 1950; myself (left) with Grp Capt 'Jamie' Jameson and Wg Cdr 'Bob' Braham.

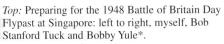

Top: Preparing for the 1948 Battle of Britain Day Flypast at Singapore: left to right, myself, Bob Stanford Tuck and Bobby Yule*.

Bottom left: I assist Lady Broadhurst with the presentation of prizes at Erwald, Austria, on conclusion of the RAF ski championships. I was at this time Captain of the Team.

Middle & bottom right: Gloster Meteor 8s of the Linton-on-Ouse Wing during the early 1950s.

Top: Another CFE group; myself (still then a Sqn Ldr), with David Atcherley, the Commandant, and Wg Cdr Al Deere.

Bottom: May 1962, the 50th birthday of 1 Squadron at Tangmere: left to right, myself, Air Cdr Philip Sanders (in the process of retirement), Air Vice-Marshal (later Air Chief Marshal) Sir Theodore McEvoy, KCB, CBE, Grp Capt Prosser Hanks and Grp Capt 'Johnnie' Walker. Note that three of us are wearing the new uniform tunics without lower pockets, which had just been introduced by Air Chief Marshal Slessor.

Top: On return from Switzerland I attended 246 Jet All-Weather Refresher Course at the RAF's Air Academy at Manby, prior to taking command of RAF Chivenor. Here I enjoy centre stage with my fellow pupils.

Middle left: Guest night at Linton-on-Ouse; I am accompanied by Nina Fosch, a ballerina who died tragically soon afterwards, and by Grp Capt Alan Anderson, the Station Commander, with Mrs Anderson.

Bottom left: Preparing to take over as Air Attaché at Berne, Switzerland; Grp Capt Peter Wickham, my predecessor, and I, with two of the Swiss Colonels. Note that Pete and I still have the fags going!

Above right: 'Billy's Bar' on the Algarve, Portugal.

Top left: With my younger son, Simon, not only an advanced ski instructor, but also one of the most well-known mountain hot-air balloonists. We are seen here in Chateau d'Oex, Switzerland.

Top right: With my sons and my elder son's wife in Switzerland.

Bottom: Skiing with my grandchildren and daughter-in-law at Gstaad, about 1992.

rockets could be, and to learn how to deliver them – and be able to pass on this knowledge to the other pilots in their units. Practice firing took place on a conveniently-located live range nearby at Goswick. At the time SLAIS formed part of 59 OTU, which was the main operational training unit for Typhoon pilots. For those of us returning from the Middle East what we were taught was not entirely new, but for all those who had been flying in Fighter Command on sweeps and bomber escorts – pure fighter work – this was all completely outside their previous experience.

At this stage we had no up-to-date aiming devices and had to learn how to achieve a reasonable degree of accuracy using our standard gunsight and judging the angle of dive into which we had entered. We were being initiated into each new phase of air warfare almost completely blind, and it was still very much a matter of trial and error. We then had to return to our units and try and teach our pilots how to follow suite. One of the biggest problems was getting them to dive steeply enough. To achieve optimum results, a dive at about 60 degrees was required. In practice most pilots feel that they are at such an angle when they have only actually achieved 40 degrees; by contrast, 60 degrees feels as if you are going down vertically. When we first led the boys into the genuine 60 degree article, they landed back at base ashen-faced by the experience – but they learned quickly.

By the end of January 1944 I had returned to SLAIS for a second course, flown mainly on Spitfires. I noted in my logbook that during a period of about two and a half months I flew 43 hours in Typhoons and 12 in Spitfires, a fair part of the former and all of the latter at SLAIS. What had been nice was to find that the commanding officer of 164 Squadron was Humph Russell, whilst one of his flight commanders was Arthur Todd, both of whom had served with me in 128 Squadron in West Africa. Indeed, Todd had been the only other pilot to gain a victory whilst with that unit.

Most of my initial flying with the Wing was done with 195 Squadron, which was led by Don Taylor until January, and then by C.A. Harris, but during February this unit was disbanded, and I transferred my personal aircraft over to 164 Squadron. Around this time 16, 20 and 22 wings had all been rechristened sectors, and the airfields had become wings in their stead. Thus 136 Airfield became 136 Wing. Following the disbandment of 195 Squadron, 193 arrived to take its place, followed in April and May by 183 and 266 Squadrons, and ultimately, in July, by 163 Squadron. We also moved from Fairlop to Thorney Island during March.

I note that during the early weeks of the year, apart from attacking the dread 'No-balls', we also undertook the occasional escort mission to medium bombers – Mitchells of 2nd TAF – and also bombed some shipping.

One of my fellow Wing Leaders was Denys 'Killer' Gillam, who led 146 Wing, and who was known to be a quite fearless pilot, who it could be quite dangerous to follow. During this period (I think it may have been about the start of April), Denys invited me to tag my wing onto his for an attack on a target at Cherbourg – then noted for the ferocity of its flak defences. Realising that we would be arriving last, when the defences were fully alerted, I was not overwhelmingly keen or enthusiastic, but we went along nonetheless.

As I anticipated, the flak was vile by the time my boys arrived, and we took a fair pasting. I landed back in a pretty foul mood, blazed into his debriefing and uttered a stream of fairly specific invective regarding his parentage, judgement, etc. Unfortunately, what I did not know was that Denys was just in the process of being promoted to Group Captain to take over command of our 20 Sector.

I was still fuming a few days later when he entered my office, and I almost ignored him. "Don't you usually stand up when a senior officer enters?" he asked me, more than a little tetchily. "Yes – but not for you!" I responded, despite taking in the fourth ring on the sleeve of his uniform! Not very diplomatic, I fear, and it may well have had something to do with the posting I received a few days later.

At this time the Fighter Leaders School (FLS) had recently moved from Chedworth in Gloucestershire to Milfield, where 59 OTU had been disbanded at the end of January 1944. In doing so, FLS absorbed SLAIS, now encompassing a Tactics Wing with three squadrons, and an Armament Wing with two squadrons. It was to this establishment that I was posted on 18 April 1944 as commander of the Armament Wing, and Chief Flying Instructor, taking over from 'Boy' Brooker, who went to lead 123 Wing. The purpose of the school was to provide instruction for all types of fighter unit leaders or potential leaders, day or night, ground attack or high altitude. This included RAF, Fleet Air Arm and USAAF pilots.

The commanding officer was a most notable fighter pilot, Grp Capt Jamie Rankin (who had just taken over from Grp Capt J.R.Adams, AFC), and I recall that one of my fellow instructors was another ex-Typhoon Wing Leader, Bill Pitt-Brown, who had also fallen foul of someone higher up the pecking order, and who I recall had been suffering some problems from varicose veins.

Jamie Rankin was a great character, and had been a very successful fighter pilot, leading the Biggin Hill Wing. Unfortunately he was one of those characters given to alcohol in a big way. Until one got to know him well, it was quite difficult to tell whether he was pissed or not, as he remained completely *compus mentis* whilst drinking, never slurring his words, or becoming aggressive. However, he gradually said less and less as the drinks went down, and once he had stopped talking, you came to realise that he was past the point of no return. Sometimes his batman would discover him next morning, still asleep in a chair somewhere in the Mess. On occasion during an afternoon he could be found downstairs in the Mess, having tea – except that the teapot was full of whiskey! This became very sad, as ultimately he lost his wife, family and career in the RAF due to his drinking, which ultimately killed him, alone and forgotten.

A few words are probably appropriate at this stage to explain both the existence and the importance of SLAIS, and FLS into which it was absorbed. The need for such a unit was based considerably upon recent past experience. Since the primary role of a fighter aircraft is to shoot down hostile opponents, facilities for perfecting a pilot's ability to operate what was in effect a flying gun as effectively as possible, should have meant that training in this skill clearly ought to have been a priority element of said training. As I have mentioned on occasion earlier in this book, in practice this had not occurred in the period between the two world wars – and indeed, had failed to occur during the opening years of World War II. Whilst this failure in the years of peace may well have had something to do with the costs involved during a period of great economic restraint, there can be little doubt that those in authority in the RAF – and certainly right down to squadron commander level in many cases – had rather lost sight of the primary purpose of the existence of their fighter aircraft. Piloting skills associated with close formation flying and aerobatics suitable for showing off at air displays took priority, although when the chips were down, these skills proved pretty worthless in the crucible of air combat. In the modern lingo, it was very much a case of "spin" overshadowing purpose.

Thus it was that between the two wars, and even during the pilot's operational training between 1939-43, there was no formal training and experience of aerial gunnery. During the peacetime period, fighter squadrons were sent to Armament Practice Camps once a year for two weeks. However, there were no professional air gunnery instructors available at these camps, and any expertise had to be self-taught without proper reference to World War I experience.

Most of the fighter pilots and aces of that war were dead, retired, or far too busy dealing with the expansion and administration of the RAF to be seriously considered as Practice Camp instructors. The situation in World War II was just as bad (if not worse), and no air firing instruction was given to pilots being converted to operational aircraft at Operational Training Units prior to their being posted to squadrons. In most instances therefore, a pilot's first experience of firing his guns was probably in an air combat situation.

The splendid Central Gunnery School existed, but its facilities were strictly limited. Indeed, initially it had been set up to train the gunners who would serve in bombers, rather than fighter pilots. In most cases a pilot only got there when he had 'shown promise' during a first operational tour – if he survived that long.

As the number of pilots gaining experience and surviving grew, so the level of expertise within units finally allowed such knowledge to be passed on to new pilots on their arrival. Needless to say however, most of such advice had to be verbal, as there was little facility available for demonstration or practice. On the other hand, as the percentage of such experienced pilots grew, they were able to watch over the 'new boys' during their initial sorties to a greater extent.

Rocket and Bomb Training
As intercepting and destroying enemy aircraft was the primary task of fighter pilots during the period 1939-42, little or no thought was given to the role of fighter aircraft once air superiority had been achieved and maintained. All concerned, both in the army and the air force, realised that fighters, with their guns, were ideal weapons for attacking and destroying ground forces, particularly soft targets such as lorries, light tanks and armoured cars, and artillery units.

The Desert Air Force, commanded by Mary Coningham, and supported by such experienced fighter pilots as Fred Rosier and Guy Carter, and their staff officers, was ideally suitable for this task and very quickly armed its Kittyhawks and Hurricanes with 250lb and 500lb bombs. It can be said that this air force was the forerunner of future tactical air forces in all the Allied theatres, and that no army could or would operate without the support of such an arm. A glaring example of the truth of such a statement was the initial success of the German Ardennes offensive at the end of 1944, which saw little or no Allied air activity due to appalling weather conditions that lasted for a dangerously long period. As soon as Allied air activities resumed, the German offensive was blunted and Hitler's final major battle in Europe was repelled and came to a humiliating and costly end.

In the meantime by 1943 Fighter Command and 2nd Tactical Air Force had taken note of the Desert Air Force's successes and tactics, and began making preparations for similar support during the forthcoming invasion of Western Europe. Apart from arming improved versions of the Spitfire to carry bombs to augment the use of their cannons, the re-equipping of units with Typhoons, fitted to carry bombs or rockets, supplemented the firepower of the new Tactical Air Force.

Although the rocket was not the easiest weapon to aim, a Typhoon could unleash a battery of what equated to six inch shells equivalent to the broadside of a modern destroyer. Multiply this by a factor of 12 or 24 (the number of aircraft in a squadron or wing) and the destructive power can well be imagined.

Fighter Command's lack of air firing facilities, referred to above, was not to be repeated in 2nd Tactical Air Force, and a special unit (SLAIS) had been formed at Milfield in June 1943 for the purposes I have already outlined. The object of these courses was to ensure that unit leaders were able to teach their flight commanders and senior pilots the best tactics for ground-attack duties before the start of the Allied invasion of Normandy. Units were then to be sent to APCs to practice these new skills.

This was achieved, and meant that the various armies had the support of well-trained, well-equipped and mobile tactical air forces ready to destroy enemy troops and equipment standing in their way, prior to D-Day. History relates the effectiveness of these air forces and the birth of a completely new concept of air/ground operations, coupled with the part played by the aircraft and their pilots.

Whilst at SLAIS, prior to its metamorphosis into FLS, I had become something of an expert at firing the new 60lb rocket projectiles with which many of the Typhoon units were now being equipped to fire. I reached a stage where I could usually put at least one rocket within five yards of a tank, or other target, every time I fired off a salvo.

I had also taken my own Typhoon, BD-?, with me to FLS on leaving 136 Wing, where my place as Wing Leader had been taken by Mike Bryan. Unfortunately, he only lasted a short time, being shot down and killed by flak on 10 June.

Despite my posting to an apparent non-operational job, I managed to 'escape' for odd days back to the Wing, to fly the occasional sortie with them. On my first return visit to Thorney Island on 29 May, I was sad to discover that Humph Russell, who had just been awarded a DFC, had been shot down the day before. He had been seen to bale out however, and all were hoping that this boded well for his survival. It did, and he was subsequently reported to be a prisoner of war.

I returned to Thorney on 15 June for a few days, on the 17th providing top cover for 164 Squadron as they made a rocket attack in the Le Havre area. In this I was joined by my Belgian friend, Mike Donnet, who was also an instructor at FLS on the Tactics Wing side, and who would become Chief of Staff of the Belgian Air Force in later years. Next day I personally dropped a pair of 1,000 lb 'cookies' on a bridge near Caen. Sadly, towards the end of July the Wing was disbanded and the various squadrons parcelled out to other wings.

As a complete change, in early July I visited 1 Squadron at Detling – my first return to my old unit since 1940 – and on the 6th flew one of their Spitfire IXs in pursuit of a V-1 – which I did not catch. By the end of July 164 Squadron had moved to French soil with its new Wing, and was based at Landing Ground B.7, Martragny, and here I joined it for another brief visit on 12 August. During the day I undertook two RP attacks with the unit, one against a trio of 88mm guns in the Falais area, and one against a chateau believed to house a Wehrmacht headquarters, in the same area.

Thus ended my operational flying career, and on 25 August I made my last flights with FLS. Indeed, by 17 August I had totalled my operational flying hours in my logbook, which amounted to:-

Hurricanes	113 hr 40 min
Spitfires	112 hr 30 min
Kittyhawks	157 hr 15 min
Typhoons	24 hr 35 min
TOTAL	408 hr 00 min

Also listed were the results which I believed I had achieved against my opposite numbers in the Luftwaffe, Regia Aeronautica and Vichy French air force, as:-

Aircraft	Destroyed	Probable	Damaged
In the air	24½	9	6
On the ground	13	3	5

CHAPTER 11

NEW WORLDS AND NEW DUTIES

A welcome period of leave followed my departure from the Fighter Leaders School, which was to be followed by something completely different. In early October 1944 I went aboard the SS *Mauretania* with Peter Brothers, a fellow fighter pilot, and Paul Walmsley, a bomber chap, and we sailed for the USA, arriving at New York on the 16th of the month. From there we travelled down to Washington, D.C., and from there to Key Field, Mississippi. We were to attend a ten-week staff course at Fort Leavenworth, Kansas, due to begin on 1 November.

The US seemed very civilised after wartime England – no blackout and all the food and drink you wanted. Wonderful! I found again, as in North Africa, that I got on very well with the Yanks, but felt the course a little strange. This was due to the fact that the USAAF was still a part of the army, and much time was spent learning how to read army field manuals! Whilst there however, I did manage to get four flights in a P-40 – the USAAF's version of my old friend, the Kittyhawk. I also got a flight in a Beech C-45 Expeditor with Group Captain George Lott, who was in command of RAF training in the States.

During my time there I got on particularly well with two fellow fighter pilots. One was 'Pete' Petersen, who had led one of the 'Eagle' Squadrons in the RAF until his own country had entered the war. The other was Dick Bong, already at that time one of his air force's top scorers, and subsequently to become the American 'Ace-of-Aces'. We frequently sat together during the course, but strangely as I recall, rarely discussed much about air fighting.

During the time I was there the German offensive in the Ardennes known as the 'Battle of the Bulge' occurred, and was followed with great interest – and initially some considerable concern – by the 1,000-odd delegates on the course. We all noted particularly that this attack, which appeared to have been well planned and prepared, achieved its initial success during a period of bad weather which grounded the Allied air forces. As soon as the weather improved, opening up the skies after about three weeks of snow and fog, the attack encountered big problems and failed.

On conclusion of the course, we returned to the UK on the *Queen Mary*, finding that this beautiful liner had been completely stripped out to carry 12,000 US troops on each trip.

Arriving home in mid January 1945, I received my next posting, which proved to be a very interesting one. I joined SHAEF Headquarters at Rheims, France, where I took up the duties of Air 1, responsible for reporting on the activities of all the Allied air forces in Europe. I had to keep the Top Brass up to date with these activities every morning, the information being displayed in the main war room, where a lot of my writings remained on the boards for years after the war. My duties included collecting relevant information morning and evening, and briefing 'Ike' Eisenhower, Arthur Tedder and 'Tooey' Spaatz personally. My immediate boss was 'Tubby' Mermagen, a fighter pilot himself at the start of the war, and now an Air Commodore. Above us was a US Brigadier who was the only Yank I ever met who was seriously anti-British – he really loathed us. Because of his attitude, I tried always to ignore him. I was to meet him again later, when serving in Japan.

The period until the end of April 1945 was not particularly memorable – a lot of hard work most of the time. During March however, I did undertake a quick weather reconnaissance over the area where the Rhine crossings by 21st Army Group were to take place. This allowed me to telephone Transport Command in England and give them the go-ahead for the despatch of the fleet of paratroop-carrying and glider-towing aircraft which spearheaded the crossings by Montgomery's troops.

One of my more satisfactory duties occurred when, with other staff officers, I helped to organise a temporary ceasefire over northern Holland via diplomatic channels, in order to allow Bomber Command to drop substantial quantities of food to the starving Dutch population. At this stage of the war the Germans were no longer in a position to feed them.

The most notable moment happened in early May however, when Grossadmiral Doenitz and a Feldmarschal arrived to discuss the signing of the surrender document. I watched this from Kay Summerby's office, next door to Ike's. (Kay was Ike's personal assistant, driver – and mistress.) The German party were escorted in by Allied officers, and ushered into Eisenhower's office, where they all snapped to attention and gave the stiff-armed Hitler salute. Ike turned to General Beddell-Smith and told him to get them outside and make it clear to them that he required them to provide a proper military salute. This they then did.

A few days later the signing took place in the war room, but was delayed for several hours at midnight, as the Russians would not agree to certain of the terms that Eisenhower had negotiated. So we sat around waiting until agreement was reached between all parties.

A little while before this historic event, Ike personally directed that I and some other RAF officers should go up to the local airfield at Rennes as quickly as possible and try to sort out a situation which was getting out of control. On arrival we discovered that a large group of British ex-prisoners of war were being flown home from Germany via this airfield, where the aircraft carrying them had landed to refuel. It rapidly became obvious to us what was going on. It seemed that no arrangements had been made to deal with this short visit. All these poor buggers wanted to do was to get out of the aircraft for a short while to stretch their legs, relieve themselves, and enjoy a few minutes of freedom after years cooped up in prison camps.

They had been met by a bunch of middle-ranking army officers who were attempting to control this mixture of officers and NCOs in a typical parade ground manner. In effect they were behaving totally insensitively and in a typically 'Colonel Blimp' manner. This treatment was, of course, the last thing that the returnees expected or wanted to receive, and they were expressing their feelings increasingly vociferously. The resident army chaps seemed to have about as much idea and tact for dealing with this very volatile group of personalities than had the Man on the Moon!

As the situation developed, someone had the sense to inform Ike and his staff, asking for guidance and instructions, as the solution was not to be found in military manuals or Standing Orders. Returning POWs, whilst normally well-disciplined, could constitute an explosive mixture of disappointment and bewilderment if not treated with some understanding, and these men needed to be placated and calmed down. As the location of this near-riot and the mode of transport was RAF, Ike reasoned that it would be sensible to let the RAF sort out the mess – and that RAF officers might perhaps be more likely to display the necessary tact and understanding to deal with the matter.

On arrival, having made our rapid assessment of the situation, we advised the resident army officers that we were taking over, and that for the sake of peace and quiet they would be well advised to make themselves scarce. All aspects of parade ground-type discipline were dropped at once, and as rapidly as we could, we organised mobile refreshment vans to start circulating around the parked aircraft and their passengers. In a further effort to make them feel welcome and at home, we then moved amongst them, bringing them up to date on the war situation and telling them as much as possible about what awaited them when they reached the UK.

Within an hour the situation had clamed down and all concerned were in a happier mood. As soon as the aircraft had refuelled, they took off again to return the POWs to be reunited with their loved ones. However, a little bit of common sense and compassion in the first place could have avoided this unhappy event.

In Rheims at this time were the remnants of the US 82nd Airborne Division, resting and recuperating after their involvement in the Battle of the Bulge. The paratroopers had gained a reputation in their own army of being ill-disciplined hell-raisers when off duty. In practice we found them to be well-behaved, and of no more trouble than any other servicemen back from a difficult time at the front.

Rheims was quite an extraordinary place as far as its bars were concerned, for it was in the heart of the Champagne district, and these were used by the local producers as a major outlet for their products, which were all open to the public. This was a most interesting and enjoyable change compared to the ordinary run of bars – provided of course, that you liked champagne.

One of Eisenhower's senior staff officers at this time was Air Marshal Sir James Robb, who had available his own Spitfire, painted overall black and carrying his four star insignia. On several occasions when I was required to undertake duties away from SHAEF, which included a number of trips to England, he kindly loaned me this aircraft. This was great, but did lead to a few slightly embarrassing situations. These tended to occur when certain RAF Station Commanders, believing it was Robb himself who was landing on their airfield, laid out the 'red carpet', only to find that a fairly junior wing commander climbed out of the cockpit.

One such trip occurred when I was ordered to fly to Luxembourg to pick up some papers which contained an apologia prepared by von Ribbentrop, the pre-war ambassador to Britain, and now classed as a Nazi war criminal. These had been written on all sorts of bits and pieces of paper, including some of the toilet variety! I picked these up and flew them to London, where I was met by Churchill's personal staff car and told to deliver them to his flat in Whitehall. Here I was agreeably surprised to be met by Churchill's daughter Mary, who presented me on arrival with a large scotch. To be fair, I had met her before, so she was not greeting a complete stranger.

My next trip was to deliver copies of the surrender papers to the appropriate authorities in Copenhagen and Oslo, and to have Vidkun Quisling arrested in the latter city. I flew to each destination in the Spitfire, and on arrival in Oslo was provided with an open BMW for my use whilst there. Ever the keen skier, I took the opportunity to drive up to have a look at the Hollenkollen ski jump which was located within the city suburbs. Whilst doing so I was involved in a traffic accident due to my ignorance of the 'priority from the right' rule prevalent in continental Europe. I still carry the scar just above the bridge of my nose.

With the close of hostilities we moved SHAEF HQ to the A.G. Farben building in Frankfurt, and while there Ike ordered me to lay on a flypast by over 2,000 aircraft from the Allied air forces for the occasion of Marshal Georgii Zukov's visit to the Headquarters (Zukov was at this time the Soviet Army C-in-C). I had just about three days to arrange this, and by the Grace of God it all went off without a major hitch.

As my stay at SHAEF approached an end, Eisenhower presented me with a photograph of himself inscribed *To Billy from Ike*. This would have been one of my most treasured possessions, but within a month it had been stolen.

CHAPTER 12

PEACETIME

With the war in Europe over, I was now posted home to join Fighter Command Headquarters at Bentley Priory in Stanmore, on the outskirts of north-west London. Here I found that the newly-arrived Commander-in-Chief was none other than Sir James Robb. I was to be Ops 1a, and I quickly realised that my main function was not to be caught out! It really was not much of a job, and in the event I was not really much of a staff officer – certainly not a born one.

Nonetheless, the RAF seemed to want to hang onto me, for in September 1945, immediately after the end of the war in the Far East, I was granted a Permanent Commission in the rank of Squadron Leader. I think the 'powers that be' agreed with my assessment of myself in the staff role however, and hoped to improve upon that, for after nine months at Fighter Command, I was sent off in March 1946 to the Royal Air Force Staff College at Bracknell, Berkshire. Here I found a considerable group of gallant officers, all totally pissed off at having dropped two ranks, as had I (we all lost our Acting ranks at the close of hostilities), and with a directing staff at the College who hadn't seen any operations, but seemed somewhat less than sympathetic towards us – or impressed by our collective experience of actual war.

Matters came to a head as a result of one exercise based upon a 2nd TAF operation in which three of us had actually taken part. Here we felt we could not go wrong, only to find that our solutions had all been heavily red pencilled by the directing staff! This led to the start of a fairly heated public debate in front of the Acting Commandant, criticising the staff for their action. The course was by now close to revolution, and fortunately the Commandant saw the point and took the appropriate action.

It will be recalled that the love of my youth, Helen, had married in Portugal before the end of the war, her husband being Vasco De Costa, who was a fellow artist. I was to see her two or three times in France thereafter, and also saw quite a lot of her mother and her amusingly alcoholic psychiatrist brother, but I now had to make other arrangements over matters of the heart – happily with some success.

Indeed, such a matter was very much in the forefront of my mind during my time at Bracknell, and I have to admit that as a result my devotion to subjects academic being thrown at us there was not quite what it might have been. So enamoured was I of my current partner at the time, that the only fellow student that I can recall being at the Staff College was my old 213 Squadron CO from 1940, Duncan MacDonald. I probably remember him as he was also deeply involved with a member of the opposite sex, having met a very nice Scottish lass whilst at Bracknell, who also had the added attraction of being seriously rich. I recall that she was a Miss Wilson (I cannot remember her Christian name), and that they got married in 1947, fairly soon after the course ended, when Duncan changed his name to Wilson-MacDonald.

I don't think the authorities approved at all of my amorous adventures, and their action upon conclusion of the Staff College course was to post me as far away as they possibly could. Of course, at that time this meant BCAir in Japan (i.e. the British Component of the Allied Forces of Occupation). Here I arrived in October 1946 as Personal Assistant to 'Boy' Bouchier, the senior RAF commander, and here I remained until June 1947.

My stay was marked in my mind mainly because whilst in Japan I gave up smoking for the first time. Otherwise, I recall playing a lot of poker and drinking fairly unlimited quantities of cheap booze. I took the opportunity to visit the atomic devastation of Hiroshima, but most of the time there remains a void in my memory. The high spot that I do recall was a farewell party at the Indian Wing, which was to be wound up on partition of their continent. They all knew very well that within months they were going to become sworn enemies, but for three days everyone got very drunk and spent much of the time swearing allegiance and eternal friendship with each other.

From Japan I was posted to Singapore, to AHQ, Malaya, as Org 1. This had nothing whatsoever to do with flying; it was all about accommodation, requiring regular liaison with Works & Bricks. I was responsible, amongst other matters, for leave centres in locations such as Kuala Lumpur, Penang, and the Cameron Highlands, and with the main armament practice camp at Butterworth.

My immediate boss was a wonderful man called Jimmy Pike, a very gallant ex-Coastal Command pilot, who despite a tremendous war record was actually a pretty lousy flier. The problems with the Communist insurgents in Malaya began whilst I was in Singapore, but had little impact on me personally. I continued to be a pretty inept staff officer, and it was generally agreed that I could neither read nor write. Well, not properly in the official manner, anyway. I think my main claim to fame during this period was that I designed and had built the nine hole golf course at Changi. I also played a lot of rugby, and did a lot of drinking. I recall that one of my contemporaries in the Mess was Neil Wheeler, a very ambitious officer who later became an Air Chief Marshal.

I also managed to get engaged whilst in Singapore, having courted a desirable ATS officer. Unfortunately, I then changed my mind, which had a somewhat unexpected consequence. The lady in question's father was a London solicitor, and whilst not seeking to bring an action for breach of promise against me, he did write to me, warning me on threat of injunction to keep away from the parts of Singapore where she was likely to be. Some chance on an island of that size!

At last I was posted home during the spring of 1949, with the hope of returning to some real flying after a break which by now was approaching five years. I was not to be disappointed. On 22 May I was posted to the Day Fighter Leaders School (DFLS) at West Raynham – the modern equivalent of my old FLS of Milfield days. This was a great posting, where I was to serve very happily for a considerable period. DFLS was at this time commanded by Wg Cdr G.A. Brown, DFC, and was a part of the Central Fighter Establishment (CFE), itself commanded by Grp Capt G.S. Bowling. The latter I recall only as being rather nondescript, and apparently with no fighter background.

The same cannot be said of George Brown, nor of the other senior instructors. These included the great night fighter pilot, 'Bob' Braham; my old 1 Squadron chum, Prosser Hanks; Hugh Verity, who had made his name landing agents in Occupied France by night; Geoff Atherton; 'Paddy' Crisham, who later became an Air Vice-Marshal; Pat Jameson, who was my immediate CO at first; and Dalley, who was later one of the test pilots on the English Electric Lightning.

DFLS was divided into a ground-attack unit, equipped with Spitfire XIVs and Vampires, and an interceptor unit with Meteors. With my experience, I commanded the ground-attack side, with Pat Kennedy, a well-decorated Irish pilot, as my deputy, while Geoff Atherton commanded the interceptors.

Geoff was a fairly rugged Australian (yes, another of them) who had risen to Group Captain in his own air force during the war, but – like myself – reverted to Squadron Leader at the end of it. This was unknown to us at the time, and boy, did he have a chip on his shoulder. He was actually a very nice chap and a very professional fighter pilot, who I admired a lot. But at first for about three months we were daggers drawn. I think there may have been an element of jealousy behind this, as I had consistently outranked him. Anyway, one night we got pissed together, had a real heart-to-heart, and thereafter were the best of pals.

At this time Fighter Command was going through its 'many-versus-many' phase, to which I shall refer in detail later. This required superior pilot skills, and Geoff insisted that the pilots he instructed be able to fly their aircraft to the limits of its performance. This included the limits of their fuel capacity, so the interceptor unit enjoyed some fairly dodgy moments.

Of the other personalities I have mentioned, Pat Kennedy rose to command RAF Marham, but was sacked for being drunk at a guest night, and Bob Braham, finding it difficult to maintain his family on RAF pay, went off to Canada to join the RCAF for twice the money!

As I have said, the ground-attack unit was still equipped in part with Spitfires, although full re-equipment with Vampires was not to be long delayed. My initial flights after my arrival, mainly to acclimatise myself and get to know the area, were made in a Spitfire XIV. On 24 June 1949 however, I made my first flight in a jet – although this was undertaken in a Meteor, rather than a Vampire.

The most noticeable difference I found to a piston-engined aircraft was the reaction of the engines to the throttles – not nearly so rapid. The immediate response was not there, and the engines required to be eased open. After that however, there were no problems. The view from the cockpit, situated in the forward nose, was much better. The tricycle undercarriage placed the aircraft in a level position from the start, which made handling on the ground far easier, whilst the take-off and landing speeds were relative to the performance and handling of the aircraft. Once in the air, one did tend to be in and out of cloud more often as the aircraft climbed so much faster, so instrument flying ability needed to be of a good order.

To me, the biggest problem was the speed with which jets consumed their fuel. You needed to be aware of the fuel status all the time, and it was important to remember that after about 45 minutes on normal internal tankage, the engines shouldn't be running any more!

After two flights in the Meteor, I made my first hop in a Vampire six days later. This was a beautiful little aircraft, docile and manoeuvrable. She was so quiet that on a long trip it became necessary to keep looking at the instruments to check that the engine was indeed still running. Like the Meteor, she had begun life as an interceptor fighter, but as later marks of the former, with uprated Rolls-Royce Derwent engines fitted, began to appear, the performance of the Vampire fell behind, and the aircraft was relegated instead to the ground-attack role.

I resumed flying the Spitfire at the start of July, but that month was to provide the opportunity to try another jet. On the 25th the soon-to-be famous American fighter and test pilot, Colonel 'Chuck' Yeager, arrived at West Raynham in a Lockheed F-80 Shooting Star. Whilst there he flew one of our Vampires and I had 35 minutes in his aircraft. Three different jet fighters in my first four jet flights – not bad going. Two days earlier as a complete change, I had flown an Anson fitted with a Zero Reader – all-weather blind flying equipment – on a trip into Heathrow. August to October brought me more and more Vampire flying as the faithful Spitfires were phased out, and by November they were pretty well gone.

Around the turn of 1950 Pat Jameson took over as CO DFLS from George Brown. During the summer Hugh Verity moved up to fill the Group Captain Operations role with the departure of Bowling, whilst with Pat's promotion, Prosser Hanks became our next commander.

During June 1950 I spent most of the month with CFE's Instrument Training Squadron, brushing up my blind flying in this unit's Meteor 7 two-seaters.

One thing which remains clear in my memory was the situation relating to the estate of the Earl of Leicester which was nearby at West Raynham, and where reputedly good shooting was to be had. There was a firm prohibition against entry onto this land however, the reasons for which I was soon to be appraised of. Some time before my arrival, one of the senior instructors then present had been that notable fighter pilot, Bob Stanford Tuck. Bob had taken it upon himself to arrange an appointment with His Lordship to see if a party of officers from CFE might be invited to a shoot – or two.

At first all appeared to go well. Bob was shown into the presence by the butler, and tea was served. Could Wg Cdr Tuck suggest the names of those officers who he proposed should form such a party? Of course he could; he suggested Bob Braham, 'Jamie' Jameson, and one or two others.

At this stage the butler re-entered, apologising for the interruption, and spoke quietly in His Lordship's ear. The latter listened, looking increasingly unhappy as he did so. Turning to Bob, he asked him to repeat the names he had just given, a request with which Bob at once complied.

A somewhat icy conversation followed, as His Lordship explained that the message he had just received from his butler concerned the contents of a telephone message just received from the Head Gamekeeper. This worthy had informed him that he had just arrested a group of RAF officers from West Raynham who were trespassing on His Lordship's land. When questioned their names had proved to be Braham, Jameson and one other! Consequently, he concluded, any invitation which had just been issued was cancelled forthwith – "Good afternoon, Tuck!"

My time at DFLS came to an end all too soon in mid April 1951, by which time I had put in 128 hours, 15 minutes on Vampires and 33 hours 35 minutes on Meteors (plus 12 hours dual); 18 hours 50 minutes on Ansons; five hours 55 minutes on Mosquitos, and of course, the 35 minutes in the F-80 – a total of 240 hours to bring my total with the service to marginally under 2,065 hours as a pilot, plus 77 hours 10 minutes dual. On my departure Prosser Hanks filled in the 'Assessment of Ability' form which was appended to one's logbooks on conclusions of such postings, and was kind enough to assess me as "Above Average" both as a fighter pilot, and in rocket-firing ability.

CHAPTER 13

METEOR WING LEADER

My next posting was no less satisfactory, for it also brought promotion to wing commander once again as I travelled north to become Wing Commander Flying at Linton-on-Ouse. This was back to interceptor work with a vengeance. I now had at my fingertips a Wing of the latest Meteors – Mark 8s in two day fighter squadrons, and Mark 11s with a night fighter unit. This was a 'plum' posting for a fighter pilot, and no mistake.

Our Sector Commander was Group Captain John Grandy, while the Station Commander was Group Captain 'Andy' Anderson, who had been a tactical reconnaissance man during the war. My two Meteor 8 squadrons were 66, commanded by Alastair Lang, DFC, and 92 Squadron, commanded by Gordon Conway, DFC; both these chaps had impressive records during the war. The night fighter unit was 264 Squadron, commanded by 'Tommy' Thompson.

Fighter Command AOC at this time was Air Marshal Sir Basil Embry, a very 'gung ho' chap, who expected quite a lot of us. In 1951 the Meteor 8 was quite the fastest thing in Britain's skies, and we thought it was 'the cat's whiskers'. We were in for a rude shock however, for in June 1950 the war in Korea had broken out, and soon thereafter we began hearing about this new Russian fighter with swept-back wings, subsequently identified as the MiG 15. This, apparently, was proving vastly superior to all the US aircraft facing it, including the F-80.

Fortunately for the United Nations forces, the Americans were just bringing into service their own swept-wing fighter, the North American F-86 Sabre, and these were shipped out to the war zone in short order to counter this new threat.

The RAF was not to send any fighter units to Korea, but the Australians had despatched a squadron of Mustangs, which during 1951 was re-equipped with Meteor 8s just like ours. Initially it was believed that the Meteor was as good as the F-86, for it could reach 40,000 feet in about the same time. Sadly, this quickly proved not to be the case in fighter-versus-fighter combat, the Meteor pilots soon admitting that they had met their match in the MiG. They were then relegated to the ground-attack role after a short period attempting to undertake the air superiority function.

This was not of immediate concern to us however, for our role was home defence, in which (shades of 1940) we did not anticipate having to face Soviet fighter aircraft. This was still before the Soviet Union possessed a serious nuclear arsenal, and the expected threat, should hostilities break out, was deemed to be large formations of Tupolev Tu 4s. These were almost identical to the USAF's Boeing B-29 Superfortress, several of which had force-landed in Soviet territory during the final days of the Pacific War, and which had been copied in almost every detail.

When the slaughter that the MiGs inflicted on US B-29s over Korea as they appeared by day is considered, I think had such attacks occurred, we would have inflicted a similar level of execution with our Meteors.

It was this concept of attack at high level by large formations of traditional bomber aircraft which had led Fighter Command to develop its 'many-versus-many' doctrine. This implied getting as many interceptors as possible into the sky and up to altitude as rapidly as could be achieved. This was fraught with danger, for it meant getting some 24 high performance aircraft off the ground more or less simultaneously, and straight up to maximum altitude without any hanging around to form up first. This could develop into a hairy old do!!

First we developed the take-off, pairs leaving the ground every ten seconds, the first pair climbing more steeply than the next, and so on, to avoid each following pair getting caught in the preceding pair's turbulence. On most occasions I was leading the first pair, but I undertook take-off in about six different positions in the formation to ascertain just how dangerous it was for the following pairs.

Having got 24 aircraft off the ground in about four minutes, often into marginal weather conditions, stage two was to get them to altitude, often through considerable cloud, but still in formation – or at least to be in formation when we arrived at the desired height. This required good instrument flying by all concerned, as otherwise the Wing could pop out of cloud, and spread all over the shop. Having achieved the desired result, it was then necessary to reverse the whole process to get back down and land.

We did have the advantage of being able to exercise against aircraft identical to our prospective opponents. We undertook numerous such exercises with USAF B-29s, numbers of units equipped with these aircraft being based in the UK at that time. The aircraft was also provided to the RAF as a stop-gap until the RAF's first jet bombers (the English Electric Canberra) became available, and here it was known as the Washington. Our practice interceptions therefore included Washington squadrons, and those equipped with the Avro Lincoln, a development of the famous Lancaster, employed usually by night.

I recall intercepting a Washington at 35,000 feet on one occasion, coming up from beneath him and closing to about 50 feet. At that point I flew into the turbulence created by the prop-wash of his four 2,000 hp engines. Boy! This flipped me right over and threw me into a spin – panic stations!

By this time fighter squadrons had given up carrying their wartime-style squadron code letters on the sides of their fuselages, and had reverted to pre-war colourful unit markings, usually in the form of patterned bars on each side of the fuselage roundel. To identify my own aircraft, WA921, I reverted to my old BD-? on the fuselage, but in addition had the whole tail unit painted bright red.

Whilst during my periods in the Desert and with 136 Wing during the war, I had prided myself on my navigational skills, but I have to admit that when at Linton they were not always what they might have been. I recall one occasion when I was leading the Wing, but became misled, I think by signals from a sector south of us. The upshot was that I led the whole formation 100 miles off course, which with the Meteor's limited endurance was pretty dangerous. By the time I realised what I had done, there was no way of getting us all back to Linton before running out of fuel. I was able to direct 92 Squadron to Duxford, whilst I led 66 towards another airfield – Waterbeach, I believe.

By the time we approached we were down to practically no fuel at all, and I had to advise the rest of the chaps that it was up to them to find an airfield and get down as fast as they could. Thankfully everyone got down alright, although I think some ran dry on the runways and could not even taxi to dispersal. It was a damn close-run thing, which could have put a rapid end to my air force career had it gone wrong to the point of losing aircraft and lives.

There were a number of changes in personalities whilst I was at Linton. During September 1951 John Grandy handed over the Northern Sector to 'Harry' Hogan, whilst command of Linton itself passed to Michael Pedley – again two more very experienced wartime fighter pilots. In May 1952 Gordon Conway left 92 Squadron, his place being taken by Sqn Ldr J.J. Jagger, DFC – an ex-bomber pilot. The newcomer was a brilliant aerobatic pilot, but this was to be his downfall. During August he put on a display for 'Gus' Walker of Bomber Command, during which he attempted to perform the Zurabatic Cartwheel – an extremely impressive but very difficult manoeuvre invented by Jan Zurakowski, at that time Avro Canada's Chief Test Pilot. Jagger's attempt failed, and he was killed instantly in the crash which ensued. It was my very unpleasant job to identify the body, which did not prove easy. In the end I could do this only from his hands, where I was able to recognise a deformity of one finger from which he had suffered for a number of years.

His place was taken by Sqn Ldr G.R. Turner, while during that same month Alastair Lang departed 66 Squadron, handing over to Dennis Usher, DFC, DFM. Another distinguished fighter pilot in a lengthening line.

We still had no swept-wing fighters of our own as 1952 came towards an end, and it looked as if we would have to soldier on with the Meteor 8 for some time to come. The prototypes of the Supermarine Swift and Hawker Hunter had flown, as had the prototypes of the Vickers Valiant and Avro Vulcan four-jet bombers, and all had been ordered into 'Super-Priority' production.

However, at about the start of 1952 the first of two Wings of Canadair-built Sabres of the Royal Canadian Air Force arrived in the UK as part of the Dominion's contribution to NATO. To fill the gap in our defences further, orders were placed with Canadair for the licence-built version of the latest F-86E for the RAF (and indeed, 66 Squadron would become the first Fighter Command unit to operate swept-wing fighters – but after my departure from the Wing). During November 1952 I flew over to North Luffenham to visit the recently-arrived Canadians, and on the 25th was lucky enough to 'cadge' three flights in a Sabre, each of 40-50 minutes duration.

Around this time there had been a lot of Meteor crashes, the reasons for these not being known at the time – particularly as most had been fatal. Everyone was starting to get worried, the cause being put down to some form of disorientation of the pilots, possibly caused by oxygen deficiency. Eventually Basil Embry called all Meteor station, wing and squadron commanders to a briefing where he delivered a very severe lecture to us all, telling us to "pull our fingers out" and find out what was going on.

Most of us had flown down to Biggin Hill to attend the meeting, and as we all prepared to depart afterwards, I saw two of our number collide at the end of the runway whilst in the process of taking off. I remember thinking "So much for the C-in-C's bollocking!" I never did find out what the end result of all this was, for my time was up, and I was soon to be posted again.

I note from my logbook that during March 1953 no less than eight entries refer to a flypast, the name of Manchester being appended to five of these. I think we were probably practising for the Queen's Coronation Flypast which was to take place over Odiham, Hampshire, on 15 July 1953. Indeed, my last recorded flight with the Wing was on one such practice on 30 March. It was with a rather heavy heart therefore that I handed over to my successor, Wg Cdr Lionel Malins – another veteran of the North African Desert, and of Kittyhawk fighter-bombers. It was therefore he who would lead Linton's 24 Meteor 8s on the day, one of the nine Fighter Command Meteor 8 Wings taking part. Those were the days.

Turning again to my logbook, my two years at Linton-on-Ouse had brought 256 hours 50 minutes on Meteor 8s, five hours 50 minutes on the Mark 7 trainer, and 35 minutes in one of 264 Squadron's night fighters. I had also added 13 hours 55 minutes in the good old Oxford, two hours 10 minutes in the Sabre, and an odd 20 minutes in a De Havilland Hornet (where did that come from, I wonder?).

As when I had left FLS in 1944, it would be a long time before I got to fly seriously again. I commenced by taking a long leave, during which I flew out to Australia as second pilot in an RAF Transport Command Handley Page Hastings in order to see my many relatives out there. My mother also travelled out to join me, and we visited the myriad generations of her prolific Irish Catholic family. We stayed for a month, and then I flew back in another Hastings during July.

The posting which awaited me was to join an organisation in Berlin known as the X Mission to the Soviet forces. There was a reciprocal right to inspect certain aspects of each other's air forces and their installations in Germany, which was a hangover from 1945. These inspections specifically had to be overt rather than covert, so it seemed to me a pretty meaningless administrative job, all form and no content.

To make matters worse, my new boss was a rather odd fish. He had been a prisoner of the Japanese since their occupation of Hong Kong in December 1941 until the end of the war in August 1945, and he clearly had a low opinion of operational aircrew. I was dismayed with this turn of events, and voiced my unhappiness to him. He obviously did not relish having a malcontent on his hands, and spoke to the AOC, which resulted in a change in my posting to 2nd TAF Headquarters at Rheindahlen to become Deputy Chief of RAF Intelligence under Air Vice-Marshal Harry Broadhurst, who was ACAS(Ops) and would become AOC with promotion to Air Marshal in 1954.

This suited my personal tastes much better, although it did bring to light once again my deficiencies in the staff role. On one occasion when shown my immediate chief's summing up of my abilities in my annual confidential report, I felt these to be pretty damaging, and I remonstrated with him, saying that I would take it up with Broadhurst personally. He then suggested that this would be a waste of my time, as he himself had been starred on the same points by the great man himself when he was SASO. I therefore let it go.

Being based in Germany placed me not too far from places where I could again indulge my passion for skiing, and I soon became Captain of the RAF Ski Team. During one training session at Erwald in Austria, I met the head representative of the RAF Ski Association, a very attractive lady called Diana Davis, who was the spitting image of Princess Grace of Monaco. I quickly ascertained that she was the daughter of Air Commodore Peter Davis, who was AOC of what remained of the London branches of the Royal Auxiliary Air Force.

One night after a few drinks with Bill Crawford-Compton, who was commanding RAF Bruggen, and some other friends in Diana's bedroom, I noticed lined up on a shelf her beautiful leather luggage, all embossed with her initials, DD. I remember remarking that it would be very easy to change these to my initials, BD, and thought no more about it. I certainly have no recollection of suggesting that if she was Diana Drake no change would be necessary to these items.

Imagine my surprise and confusion then, when I appeared for breakfast next morning, to be widely congratulated on my engagement, with questions about when 'the happy day' would be! I was mystified, and when she appeared I asked her what they were talking about. "If you don't recall, Billy, why should I enlighten you?" was her response. I did gather however, that it had been generally concluded that my remarks of the previous night had been construed to be a proposal of marriage. I thought about this – after all, I was pushing 40 and had never been married, and she was extremely attractive, and did not appear to be responding adversely. So I asked her how she felt about the idea, which she replied should have been obvious, so we decided to go for it – just like that! Not perhaps the most promising grounds for entering into so serious and important an arrangement.

Her organising skills were considerable, so I left all the arrangements to her, including setting up a first meeting with her father. He had by this time retired from the RAF, and now owned the Starboard Club at Seaview on the Isle of Wight. The first time I met him I was slightly startled when he demanded to know whether my intentions were honourable or not. I looked him straight in the eye and said: "Being an officer and a gentleman, I do not consider such a question to be necessary." He immediately grasped my hand, offered me a large whiskey, and responded: "That's really what I wanted to know."

We got married while I was still stationed in Germany, and as my official married quarters were not immediately ready to be taken over, we were loaned those of Air Vice-Marshal Edwardes-Jones (my old CO in 6 OTU in 1940) for the first couple of weeks, which was extremely kind of him. My best man was my oldest and dearest friend, Killy Kilmartin, who was also still in the air force, and serving with Fighter Command. Diana had no intention of waiting long for a family, and our first son, Dayrell, was born at the RAF Hospital at Wegburg on 1 April 1956. His two godfathers were John Grandy and Peter Ottewill. The latter was another of the pre-war Tangmere boys, having been a Sergeant Pilot with 43 Squadron in those days. He and I had become good friends during my time with 2nd TAF, where he was serving as a staff officer.

My tour came to an end in summer 1956, and we prepared to return to England. My flying during the past three years had been just sufficient to retain my flying pay, and involved mostly local flights in Ansons and Vampires, though I did manage to get a couple of flips in a Percival Prentice trainer, and one in a De Havilland Venom, the Vampire's successor in RAF Germany, as 2nd TAF's controlling body had now become. This one hour hop was to be the only experience of this nice little aircraft which I was to get.

Back in England I was sent first to the Flying College at RAF Manby on a refresher course. This lasted only about a week, and was spent almost entirely in a Meteor 7 with a Flt Lt Hester, honing my instrument skills. There was one particular highlight however, for on the 10th I got my first flight in a Hawker Hunter, this beautiful aircraft now being fully established in service with RAF squadrons by this time. My 35 minute flight was actually in a Mark 2, which was powered by an Armstrong Siddeley Sapphire engine, rather than the Rolls-Royce Avon which the initial – and the later – versions employed.

This was but a 'taster' however, for I was not to receive a flying job at this stage, going instead to Horsham St Faith, to the Headquarters of Fighter Command's Eastern Sector, as Fighter Controller for the area. Once again my flying would have to be gleaned wherever possible to keep up that flying pay to help keep my family.

My time at Horsham was not particularly memorable, being just what the job indicated – controlling other fighter pilots whilst they did the flying. I generally managed one or two flights a month, usually in either a Meteor (Mark 7 or 8 – whichever was available) or in one of the faithful old Ansons. On 5 April 1957 I managed to get a few more shots at a Hunter; my first two flights were in a Mark 5, which coincidentally like the Mark 2 was also Sapphire-powered, but the third and final trip was in one of the latest Avon-powered Mark 6s, which was a considerably more powerful machine than the earlier versions, with a substantially higher performance.

1957 was also marked by the birth of our second son, Simon, on 8 December. During August 1958, as my time with Eastern Sector approached its close, I did a concentrated month's flying on the Hunter 6, totalling 22 hours 30 minutes, bringing my overall total of flying hours to 2,689 hours, 55 minutes. I believe that this was to prepare me for my next posting, which was to be as Air Attaché to Switzerland, as the Swiss had recently acquired the export version of the Hunter 6 for their air force.

I found the Hunter a delightful aircraft to fly, reminiscent of the Spitfire. It was very light on the controls, which were hydraulically actuated, and it could be quite amusing to watch a pilot making his first solo on the type, the aircraft gently 'fluttering' from side to side as he got the feel of the controls.

One did need to be completely aware of the procedures to get out of a spin, which had become clear after Neville Duke, Hawker's Chief Test Pilot, had suffered an accident at Thorney Island. To recover it was necessary to have the control stick absolutely centralised, and a white streak marker was added in the cockpit against which the stick should be aligned in such circumstances.

Consequently pilots were advised to do one spin to gain the experience of recovery, but generally to refrain from doing so again. I was not impressed with this suggestion, and spun the Hunter on every chance I got – but that was just me.

It was also very necessary to attach the lower legs of one's flying suit to two buckles at low level on the seat. If it became necessary to eject, these operated to pull the legs in close, as otherwise they could be caught on the rear edge of the windshield when ejecting, with extremely unpleasant consequences. Look . . . no kneecaps!!

The four big 30mm Aden guns really thumped when fired, and if attacking a ground target one had to be careful not to be distracted by this, as it was very easy to fly straight into the ground. I never had a chance to fire them at an air-to-air target, so cannot comment regarding how they performed in this respect.

CHAPTER 14

AIR ATTACHÉ

So it was that, newly-promoted Acting Group Captain, I arrived in Berne to take over the job of Air Attaché from Pete Wickham. As Group Captains we were on an equal rank footing with the officers of the Swiss army and air force, all of whom were Colonels in times of peace. The family accompanied me, and we were provided with a lovely house on the outskirts of the city. Sadly however, my marriage was beginning to slide downhill at this time, although it would just about survive our stay in Switzerland.

Being in this Alpine country did mean that we could ski virtually every weekend through much of the year, and this helped. With parentage such as they had, our sons had little chance but to become accomplished skiers. Indeed, soon after our arrival I took Dayrell down the slopes on my back!

Shortly after I had established myself, I was taken aside by one Swiss Colonel and appraised of what was expected of me. Switzerland, he emphasised, was a strictly neutral country, and espionage of any sort against them would have to be dealt with equally as severely be it East or West that was involved. If I wanted to know something, I should ask through the proper channels, and wherever possible, I would be told the answer.

He also described to me the strength of rumour in such an environment. He had decided during the war to see just what could be the effect of rumour amongst other military attachés in a neutral country. He therefore set up a large map of Turkey, on which he showed all the larger Turkish units steadily being moved from their southern frontiers with Iraq, Iran and Greece, to their northern frontier with the Soviet Union. Each time he moved a unit in this way, he told one of the other attachés in the *strictest secrecy*, then waited to find what use that attaché made of the information. Finally he was approached by the British Military Attaché to ask if he knew about the redeployment of the Turkish army – the whispering had gone full circle!

It is not always recognised that during World War II the Swiss army disliked the Germans intensely. In summer 1940 German aircraft had on several occasions infringed the sovereignty of Swiss airspace, leading to some quite considerable aerial combat. The most successful of the Swiss fighter pilots, now a Colonel, became a close friend of mine whilst I was there, and recounted to me a story connected therewith.

In a time when war is a possibility, one of the Colonels is selected to become a General and Chief of the Army, for the duration. The General so appointed had become aware that the Germans had prepared contingency plans for the invasion and occupation of Switzerland. Whilst Switzerland maintains only small standing forces, every able-bodied male receives military training, and thereafter retains his uniform and weapons at home in readiness, so that the forces which can rapidly be mobilised represent a particularly high percentage of the national population.

The General called for a meeting with his Wehrmacht opposite number (von Rundstedt, I believe) and without more ado presented him firstly with a copy of the German's own proposals, followed by a copy of the Swiss plans for their own defence against such an eventuality. These effectively amounted to a 'scorched earth' policy, which the German officer quickly agreed would require a scale of force of circa 30-35 divisions to secure so small and relatively unimportant a country, due to its demanding geography. He had to concede that such an attempt would be unwarranted.

My having been educated in Switzerland at a school where a lot of Swiss politicians had also attended, helped me a lot, and I was always treated very well, and I thoroughly enjoyed my time there. I managed to remain completely neutral myself and found that they were as good as their word – any information I wanted, I could almost always obtain through the correct channels.

My most unsatisfactory experience whilst Air Attaché arose not from the Swiss or any of my opposite numbers, but from our own politicians. At that time the Swiss were considering the need eventually to replace the Hunter in service with their air force, and were evaluating a number of European and US fighters as possible candidates. At one period they had decided upon the French Dassault Mirage, but were investigating the possibility of having this aircraft re-engined by Rolls-Royce, with its hydraulics by Dowty – both British companies. This would result in a lot of the work coming to Britain, rather than the whole order going to France.

Negotiations had reached a government-to-government level, and the decision had come to a stage where much depended on the Royal Australian Air Force, which was also considering a similarly-equipped version of the Mirage, thus providing an economy of scale. This caused me to be in constant touch at this point with Frank Carey, Rolls-Royce's representative in Australia, who had been with 43 Squadron at Tangmere in 1939, when that was 1 Squadron's sister unit.

As it became obvious that the Australians were losing interest in the idea, the Swiss sought to obtain the best terms which the British government would offer in order to achieve such a deal with them alone. It was anticipated that such terms would ultimately be substantially more favourable than the figures initially submitted. I had my doubts whether the British government of the day would have the will to secure the transaction, and warned my Swiss contact, the Chief of the Air Staff, accordingly.

A high level meeting was arranged, and Reggie Maudling, then the Minster responsible, came over from London with his advisers to brief the Swiss Prime Minister (who was also the Minister of War) on the best terms that could be offered. Maudling then spent a long evening with the British Ambassador, drinking rather heavily and reminiscing, only getting to bed about 4 a.m.

The Swiss like to make an early start to the day, and the meeting had been called for 8 a.m., so it was a bleary-eyed Minister who arrived with his Civil Service adviser, a gentleman named Havilland, and myself. Upon sitting down, the Prime Minister asked him directly what the British offer was, and Maudling specified a figure which was in fact that which had originally been offered, and which had actually been considerably improved upon in an effort to secure the contract. I saw Havilland's eyes rise to heaven in despair. The Prime Minister then stated icily that this figure was at a significant variance with recent official offers that had been received from the British government, and that therefore the meeting was at an end. Those offers had in fact been much closer to the final figure which Maudling should have presented.

I was then called to a gloomy meeting with the Swiss Chief of the Air Staff, where I was told that they were not going ahead, but were going to purchase the all-French Atar-powered Mirage. All that was left to me was the sad satisfaction of saying: "I told you so."

I had been very surprised by the selection procedure however. Although the Swiss were very thorough in their methodologies, they had not had a single recognised current aviator on the selection committee. Because the air force was a part of the army, it was not considered inappropriate that all the army men were from the artillery – mainly the anti-aircraft branch – and they were considered just as qualified to select an aircraft as a pilot. The only pilot involved was very elderly and quite out of date, with little or no understanding of modern jet aviation.

On a lighter note, I also got to know Bill Lear Junior well whilst in Switzerland, where he was very interested in getting his Learjet company aircraft manufactured under licence. As a consequence he had got to know the local aviation industry well, and managed to wangle us a chance to fly the Pilatus P-16, a nationally-designed and built jet fighter prototype, which although being quite a good aircraft, never went into production.

On the appointed day I went with him in his private Cessna, which he had equipped with every piece of electronic equipment used in the Learjet. He went up first in the P-16, but made such an awful landing that it was not then available for me to fly. So after a very good lunch, we flew home again.

It was a quirk of the Air Attaché scene here, that several nationals – but particularly the Russians – were keen to serve in the post as long as possible, and by virtue of such long service become the 'doyen' of the attachés. I had been earmarked to take command of RAF Chivenor on my return to the UK, but for a variety of reasons this posting was not to become available until June 1962. I was in no hurry to leave Switzerland, so did nothing to rock the boat, with the result that I remained in post for three and a half years, during the final months outstripping all the others in the length of my stay, and thereby it was I who became the 'doyen'!

I therefore returned to England at the end of April 1962, and spent the next month on No 246 Jet All-Weather Refresher Course at Manby, before taking over Chivenor, pleasantly situated in North Devon, where the Hunter Operational Conversion Unit was based. Manby was once again Meteor 7s and 8s, but Chivenor was to be all Hunters, both Mark 6s and the Mark 7 two-seat trainer, which I had not flown before.

My return had a sourer note however, for by this time Diana had told me that she wanted a divorce. In those days divorce by agreement was virtually impossible – there had to be blame, or evidence of unreasonable behaviour. Ever the officer and gentleman, fool that I was, I agreed to go through the sordid charade of producing 'evidence', arranging a hotel room, a paid tart and a photographer to record my 'misconduct'. This all occurred during the time I was at Manby, so I did not arrive at Chivenor in the most ideal state of mind to take on the duties of Station Commander for the first time.

Thus, when inside a year of my new command commencing, I had a talk with Al Deere, who was in charge of promotions from Group Captain to Air Commodore. Being an honest guy and a fellow fighter pilot, Al showed me a list of my contemporaries and asked me frankly if I thought I could read and write as well as those buggers! I had to agree that the answer was no; I was an active air force officer, only really interested in flying. He agreed, and so I asked him to put me forward for premature retirement so that I could get involved in some other career whilst there was still time.

In retrospect I could not have timed this worse, for I did not realise that the forces' pay structure was even then under review. Had I stayed on for a couple more years I would have obtained a far better pension than I actually got. But then in those days few of us even considered such matters, and there was little enough advice available. Therefore in July 1963, after nearly 30 years in the Royal Air Force, my life was about to change completely – and without a wife and family to share it with me. And I would never get to fly an aircraft again.

CHAPTER 15

LIFE ON THE OTHER SIDE OF THE WALL

So I entered my new life, as I now realise sadly ill-prepared for what I was to find there. Cocooned by the service, I was at that stage still little more than a young fighter pilot – although now aged 45.

For the first six months I lived in London, deciding what to do with the rest of my life. During this period I was introduced to a businessman by a solicitor friend of mine, with whom I seemed to develop a good rapport. Quite soon after we had met, he offered me the job of Personal Assistant Designate and Export Manager, to take control of a firm which he was intending to launch onto the market. This, he advised me, would take another six to eight months to achieve. He suggested that I should take a good holiday in the interim.

This seemed like early good fortune – just the job in fact. Off I went to Switzerland to get some skiing in, and whilst there I was told that I should see Portugal, a country of which I knew nothing. I therefore telephoned my current girlfriend in London and advised her that I would not be coming back directly to England, as I intended to move on to Portugal to await the call to commence my new career. Had she ever heard of Portugal, I asked? Well, by chance, yes she had, because her ex-boyfriend had just asked her to go out there and buy some properties for him. So we duly arranged to meet in that country.

On arrival I found the Algarve area in the south of the country to be very much to my taste. At that time it was also little developed and very cheap, and I therefore invested some of the gratuity which I had received on my departure from the air force, in some property, the rents from which would help to keep me going nicely in the meantime.

Having sorted myself out in this seemingly satisfactory manner, I wrote to my prospective employer in London to ask him how things were going, and when I should present myself for duty. Within a week I received a letter from his newly-widowed wife to tell me that John had been found dead with his head in a gas oven. End of prospective career.

My investment in the Algarve proved to have been a good one however. I had actually purchased two brand new blocks of apartments, one of eight and one of five, plus a ground floor shop. Initially therefore, I sold four of those in the first block, and the capital so realised was sufficient, together with the rents from the others, to live on for the next two or three years. I also lived in one of the apartments in the second block. All were located in Faro, in a good neighbourhood, and handy for the airport.

During this period I encountered Inge, a German lady who had previously been the girlfriend of a well-known Canadian novelist called McKenzie, who had made his name mainly by writing a story based upon the robbing of expensive homes in the South of France.

Inge was from an aristocratic family which had originated near the Belgian border; she was a 'Von'. She had in the past been married to a banker, and had two children from that earlier union. Her father and uncle had once owned a very large steel concern near Bonn, but whilst the former had been away in the army during the war, his brother had managed to rob him of his inheritance. Consequently, the two never spoke again.

He was a large, tall man who had in the past drunk a lot of beer, although he had given this up in recent years. We got on well together, but there must have been some question regarding his overall abilities, for despite his family background, not only did he lose his share of the family firm to his brother, but throughout his military service on the Eastern Front, he never received a commission, his highest rank being that of Oberfeldwebel (Staff Sergeant).

Inge and I just clicked immediately, which was to prove unfortunate, as we rapidly decided to get married. To arrange this quickly, we sought a licence in Gibraltar, where the Governor proved to be an old friend of mine, Admiral Mike Fell, and ex-Fleet Air Arm fighter pilot, who I had known for years. I asked him if he would sponsor me, which he readily agreed to do, so we had dinner and stayed in a famous hotel on 'The Rock' while the permission came through. Mike very kindly laid on a reception for us aboard an Arctic survey ship which was refitting in the harbour there, and also acted as my best man. Inge was suitably impressed by my impeccable contacts!

By now the Algarve was becoming a popular holiday destination. A lot of people in England were buying properties as investments to let, or as holiday homes which could also be let out when not in use by the owners. This created a new opportunity to manage and look after such properties for them, and to exploit this situation Inge and I set up business together, which lasted for some years.

Unfortunately on a personal level we only remained on good terms for about two years, following which we began to fall out to an increasing degree. She demonstrated a dogmatic Teutonic pigheadedness which in the end I just could not stomach. Our marriage actually lasted seven years in total, but during the latter part we had separated, although we continued to run the business together. Meanwhile the business had proved very lucrative, and we had purchased a house, out of which I now had to move.

Fed up with this situation, I therefore returned to England, where I sought out 'Paddy' Barthropp, another old fighter pilot pal, who was now running a pretty up market car hire organisation in Kensington, and asked him to give me a job. He therefore took me on as one of his drivers, and for the next 18 months or so I chauffeured the well-heeled of London around the capital, first in a Volvo, and then in a Rolls-Royce or Daimler stretch-limo.

This didn't seem to be getting me anywhere fast however, and ultimately I chucked it in and returned to Portugal. By now I had sold the remaining apartments in the first block to keep me going, although I retained the second block, which was now fully let. I therefore moved into one of the flats that the firm was managing, which did not greatly recommend itself to Inge. It was during this period that I was taken seriously ill, cerebral meningitis being diagnosed. I was rushed to hospital in a pretty dire condition and in very considerable pain. Here I discovered that the ministrations of the devoted of the Roman Catholic faith did not seem to have improved greatly in their care and consideration from that meted out to me by the Brothers so many years before. The nuns provided me with precisely one aspirin a day, and left me to suffer. There was damned little comfort given.

As soon as I could travel, I was shipped back to England, to the RAF Hospital at Wroughton. Here I was given a thorough check-up, and was declared cleared. One of the aftermaths of this episode was an attack of severe depression, but one good thing came out of this – I gave up alcohol, and have never returned to it.

By the time that all this was sorted and I got back to Faro, my marriage to Inge was at an end. I was also fairly broke, and on the lookout for opportunities. At this stage I met a fellow Englishman who seemed quite interested in my block of apartments, and particularly in the shop that it incorporated. He expressed a desire to start a business there to sell under-floor central heating, and showed me a letter of intent from a firm in England which would supply the equipment.

I pointed out that I had no money, but that I did have the property and my local contacts, which he appeared to accept as my collateral. Therefore, on a shake of hands we became partners. Innocent that I then was, it never occurred to me to require a proper written agreement of terms and liabilities.

Of course, I know little or nothing whatsoever about the business, but the idea was that I would be responsible for drumming up the orders, and he would undertake the installations. He was a pretty hard-headed businessman, but he put up the initial capital for equipment, stock, etc, as I had anticipated. My lack of knowledge and selling skills soon became obvious, and the whole enterprise started to disintegrate. He quickly realised that I was not up to it and blamed me for its failure, demanding that I should recoup him with the capital he had invested, and shares in the business which he said he wanted to give to his son. I only had a few shares, and handed these over, but had no money to repay him his capital. In the event we argued about this for a year or so before he finally got the message and went away.

This experience made me realise that in this world you just do not go into business without financial and legal advice. I had only just started to grow up since leaving the RAF, and as my next experience was to show, I still tended to be far too trusting.

Now it was that I met my final 'bêtes noir' in the shape of an American couple who were looking to acquire a pub. I was introduced as someone who knew what was likely to be available in the Albufuera area. I therefore went to talk to the local Managing Director of the Westminster Property Group, which was at that time very active in the Algarve as a developer. The MD, a gentleman named Edwards, had been in the RAF, and had at one time been PA to Air Marshal Sholto Douglas. We had lost touch after Cairo in 1943, but I had recently met him again in Portugal, purely by chance and socially.

His group had developed a supermarket property, which included a shop (at that time empty), with a first floor above which there was the potential for a nice restaurant. I thought the American couple could be persuaded to sponsor me to run such an establishment, and Edwards agreed that it could easily be converted into a pub.

In this way 'Billy's Bar' was born. We took a lease, and the Westminster people undertook the works necessary. Within three months we had a bar and restaurant operating as a going concern. The American wife was a fairly accomplished cook, and ran the restaurant upstairs, concentrating on fast food, while I ran the bar and her husband looked after the books.

We had fully stocked the bar and cellar, and everything operated very nicely until the season ended, around the end of October. In November the male member of the pair, who it had turned out was a professor of art at home, announced that they were going back to the States.

I was aghast! He had previously stated that he intended to stay in the Algarve for the rest of his life. There was now no talk of funding continuing, and whilst the business supported itself during the summer, there had not yet been sufficient profit generation to maintain it during the winter period. So off they cleared to Washington, and I was left to do a round of my local friends to get sufficient cash to cover the next five months or so until the holidaymakers returned. I had to borrow about £8,000-£9,000, with no real collateral.

When the next season started the pair did have the good grace to return, but it quickly became obvious that they had no intention of financing the project correctly, and expected me to render it self-supporting. For the first time I found myself in the unenviable position of being snarled at by people who had let me down! As soon as the season ended, off they went again, back to Washington.

By the time the third season arrived, they had brought in a partner, and it was he who came over this time. It was soon abundantly clear that they had not put him properly in the picture, but he was one of the hard-nosed type of Americans, and rapidly started telling me what we were going to do and not do, at which I pretty quickly jibbed. I demanded that he repay all the borrowings that I had been obliged to incur on the couple's behalf, and at that he lost interest and soon cleared off back to the States.

By now we had managed to struggle by for three years, supported at least morally by Edwards, who had been a real friend. At this stage however, he died, and the group went into decline – certainly as far as its presence in Portugal was concerned. The new Managing Director was little interested, and obviously was looking for as few headaches as possible. The American 'partners' had now all disappeared, and from that time onwards the Westminster people were trying to get me out.

In fact I did manage to keep the show on the road for several more years, working in the bar during the summer and playing golf solidly throughout the winter months. In the end however, it all became unsustainable, and I handed over my remaining property interests in such payment as I could make towards the accrued debts, closed up, called it a day, and came home to England in 1993.

Here then I have been for nearly ten years, living in a small apartment in Kensington. I was able to invest in a Toyota Previa 'people carrier', and entered into an arrangement with a travel firm by which I collect and deliver foreign visitors between the airports and their hotels during the mornings, with such other journeys as I may be called upon to undertake.

My younger son, Simon, now lives with his family in Switzerland, where he is an advanced ski instructor, and a recognised mountain balloon pilot. So every year I get a month or so on the piste, indulging in my lifetime passion. I have also taken part in various fighter pilot seminars here and in the USA with a varying degree of interest and enthusiasm.

I realise as I look back that I only really began to grow up and come to terms with the world when I left the service. I have lived my life very much off the cuff and as it comes, and whilst interesting, it has not always been easy.

Per Ardua ad Astra

CHAPTER 16

RETROSPECT

The aspect of my service in the Royal Air Force which still impinges most forcibly upon my consciousness is how different its ethos and its methods of carrying out its functions were from those of the other, more traditional arms of service – the army and the navy. I have already referred briefly to this phenomenon in Chapter 3, but am drawn back to it here.

At the highest levels of command, the generals and admirals were usually, like the air marshals, tucked away far behind the lines in their headquarters, planning the grand strategies, issuing directives and orders – and placating the politicians! However, not so far below them were the fleet and army commanders, who were much closer to the fighting units – the 'sharp end' – and indeed, were often right there with them. The subaltern in command of a platoon, the captains, majors, and indeed, the lieutenant colonels and brigadiers, were usually in the thick of the action, they and their NCOs leading the men who made up the bulk of the fighting force.

Similarly, officers from the lieutenants and commanders who commanded the crews of the MTBs, frigates and destroyers, the captains who were in charge of the larger warships – the cruisers, battleships and aircraft carriers – and the rear admirals, when fleets were involved, all played their part when action was joined. Again however, whilst they and their immediate subordinates provided the leadership, guidance and example, the greater part of the actual fighting was done by the far larger numbers of ordinary seamen.

True, the armies and fleets all had their administrative and supply 'tails', which included large numbers of essentially 'non-combatants', who often outnumbered the 'sharp end' by a considerable factor. Nevertheless, the fact remains that officers and NCOs up to quite senior levels and of relatively advanced age were involved in the fighting on a regular basis, alongside much larger numbers of privates, able seamen and junior NCOs.

This did not apply to the air forces in the main, certainly insofar as

World War II was concerned, although to a slightly lesser extent at other times ever since combat in the air first commenced. In terms of speed of reflexes, senior officers, or those of greater age, were generally considered too slow and old to fly modern operational aircraft to their limits. They were thought to be more of a liability in action than their past experience might appear to warrant. Indeed, those who had flown throughout the 1920s and 30s, when flying 'beautifully' was the order of the day, proved to be at a particular disadvantage when war came, when the need to throw the aircraft around violently and with total abandon became necessary to survive in a dogfight.

The majority of these older officers at that time were the first to agree with these facts, and were content to leave flying fighters to their younger colleagues. Anyone over the age of 30 was considered by most of us to be nearing the limit. 'Sailor' Malan was an exception, and had reached and exceeded this limit when leading the Biggin Hill Wing. The average age of wing leaders and squadron commanders was by then in the early 20s, and even these had to be relieved from operational duties every six to nine months.

Over-confidence was the chief enemy should these timescales be exceeded; squadron and station medical officers were very conscious of these limitations and were responsible for keeping the appropriate authorities aware of the operational fitness and morale of the aircrew.

Of course, as in any situation, there were exceptions. Pilots like Victor Beamish and Harry Broadhurst were not to be kept out of the air if they could help it. However, as a general rule officers of group captain rank were actively discouraged from flying on operations, even amongst those who as a consequence of their experience and expertise had reached such rank at a relatively early age. A few of the pilots promoted to command, rather then to lead wings late in the war (such as Denys Gillam) did continue to fly operationally as group captains, but they were very much in the minority.

The advent of power controls, radar aids, etc has somewhat ameliorated this situation in more recent years, and experience has become a much more predominant factor. Certainly this was already evidenced by the number of World War II pilots who did well in Korea, even with the early jets, whilst wars such as those in Vietnam and the Falklands have witnessed outstanding performances by fighter pilots far older than we would have thought possible back in the 1940s.

The main difference between air forces compared with armies and navies, however, is in the composition of the 'sharp end' to an even greater extent than the age and rank of the officers involved. To fly an aircraft adequately has always required a relatively high degree of intelligence and ability. This goes too for most other airborne duties aboard night fighters, bombers, reconnaissance or coastal patrol aircraft. For this reason pilots – and to a considerable extent, specialists such as navigators and radar operators – whether initially they were officers or senior NCOs – are all at least potentially 'officer material'. In several air forces all pilots were always officers as a matter of course; in the RAF they have always been of at least sergeant rank. Early in the war, air gunners were frequently junior 'other ranks' who volunteered for this additional duty. Before the war was a year old it had been realised that such men required specialised training; they also needed protection from being directed onto other more mundane ground duties by over-officious senior NCOs, when they should be resting or preparing between operations. Consequently, all aircrew became sergeants at least. This also ensured rather better treatment should they be unfortunate enough to become prisoners of war.

Consequently, the vast majority of air force personnel, including all ranks from junior NCO downwards, were effectively 'non-combatants'. Many were craftsmen, skilled in their trades, but all formed a huge administrative, supply and support tail to the very small sharp end, which was composed entirely of those who, in the other services, would be the leaders.

Only on the rarest of occasions would such ground personnel be called upon to fight, and then only in a pseudo-army manner if their airfields were in danger of being overrun. These ground crews were vital to the effective operations of the squadrons of which they formed a part, and were generally kept extremely busy, servicing the aircraft and the aircrews; as skilled men they had little time for anything else. The need therefore to provide army units for the protection of airfields was something which always rankled with Winston Churchill, who found it difficult to understand why ground crews could not be trained to be infantrymen when the need arose. The conflict which existed between their important main function and the training and fitness levels necessary to fulfil a fighting role, was something which he found difficult to comprehend. Only the formation of the RAF Regiment to fulfil this role finally brought an end to his complaints.

However, the fact remains that on, say, a typical fighter squadron in Fighter Command or 2nd TAF, personnel strength might typically run into three figures, whilst the number of pilots would normally average between 12 and 20.

In my view the modus operandi of an air force which I have sought to describe here, ensures that its whole ethos from top to bottom tends to be totally different in its nature from most other types of military or naval organisation. This has undoubtedly caused friction and lack of understanding between air forces and their sister services in the past, when the latter have sought to judge the behaviour and activities of the former on the basis of their own practices and experiences. However large an air force may become, its 'sharp end' must always in effect be more akin to what we now refer to as 'Special Forces', rather than to more traditional formations. Well-selected and trained aircrew by their very nature represent a corps d'élite. That certainly was in line with my own experiences of service, and I remain very proud to have been a part of such an organisation.

APPENDIX I

GROUP CAPTAIN BILLY DRAKE, DSO, DFC & BAR, DFC (US)

Royal Air Force Record of Service

July 1936 – 3 September 1936	Air Service Training, Hamble
22 October 1936 – 22 May 1937	6 FTS, Netheravon
22 May 1937 – 8 September 1939	1 Squadron, Tangmere
8 September 1939 – 12 May 1940	1 Squadron, Le Havre, Orchey-le-Bois, Vassincourt, Berry-au-Bac
19 June 1940 – 1 October 1940	6 OTU, Sutton Bridge
3 October 1940 – 23 October 1940	A Flight, 213 Squadron, Tangmere
24 October 1940 – February 1941	421 Flight, Gravesend, Biggin Hill, West Malling, Hawkinge (91 Squadron from January 1941)
February 1941 – September 1941	53 OTU, Heston
October 1941 – March 1942	128 Squadron, Freetown, Sierra Leone, West Africa
April 1942 – May 1942	260 Squadron, Middle East
June 1942 – January 1943	112 Squadron, Middle East
January 1943 – June 1943	HQ, Middle East and 203 Group, Middle East
15 June 1943 – October 1943	Krendi Wing, Malta
December 1943 – April 1944	136 Airfield Wing
April 1944 – September 1944	Fighter Leaders' School, Milfield
October 1944 – January 1945	US Command and General Staff School, Fort Leavenworth, Kansas
February 1945 – March 1945	School of Administration, Hereford
March 1945 – June 1945	SHAEF HQ, Rheims, Frankfurt
June 1945 – March 1946	HQ, Fighter Command, Bentley Priory, Stanmore
March 1946 – September 1946	RAF Staff College, Bracknell
October 1946 – June 1947	BC Air, Japan
June 1947 – April 1949	AHQ, Malaya, Singapore
22 May 1949 – April 1951	Day Fighter Leaders' School, CFE, West Raynham
April 1951 – April 1953	Wing Leader, RAF Linton-on-Ouse HQ, 2nd TAF, Rheindahlen
1956	RAF Flying College, Manby

1956 – 1958	HQ, Eastern Sector, Fighter Command, Horsham St. Faith
1958 – April 1962	Air Attaché, Berne, Switzerland
May 1962 – June 1962	246 Jet All-Weather Refresher Course
27 June 1962 – July 1963	Station Commander, RAF Chivenor

APPENDIX II

CLAIMS AGAINST ENEMY AIRCRAFT
FROM MY LOGBOOK

1 Squadron
1940

Date		Type	Location	Aircraft	Serial
15 Apr		Bf 109	over the lines	in Hurricane	L1590 P
„		Bf 109 unconfirmed	over Metz		
10-13(*) May	3	Do 17s		in Hurricane	
	¹/₂	He 111		„	
		Do 17 unconfirmed	over Rethel	„	

213 Squadron

10 Oct		Bf 109 Probable		in Hurricane	

421 Flight

20 Nov		Do 17 Damaged		in Spitfire I	S
6 Dec	¹/₂	Do 17Z Probable	off France	„	U
27 Dec	¹/₂	Do 215		„	I

1941

7 Jan	¹/₂	Ju 88 Damaged	off Dover	„	
„		Ju 88 Damaged	off Dover	„	

128 Squadron

13 Dec		Martin 167F		in Hurricane	BD897

112 Squadron
1942

6 Jun		Bf 109F	Bir Hacheim	in Kittyhawk Ia	AL161 GA-?
12 Jun		Bf 109 on ground		„	„
„		Bf 109 Damaged on ground		„	„
17 Jun	3	Bf 109s on ground	Gazala No.2	„	„
2 Jul		Bf 109E Probable		„	ET510 GA-Q
8 Jul		Bf 109E	LG 106	„	ET790 GA-?
23 Jul		MC 202		„	GA-Q
24 Jul		Bf 110		„	ET524 GA-X
„		Bf 110 on ground		„	„
„		Bf 109E on ground		„	„
1 Sept	2	Ju 87s		„	EV165 GA-?
13 Sept		Bf 109F		„	EV168 „
„		Bf 109F Damaged		„	„ „

107

Date		Type	Location	Flown	Serial	
1 Oct		Ju 87			„	„ „
„	1/2	Ju 87			„	„ „
„		Ju 87 Probable			„	„ „
22 Oct		Bf 109F Probable		in Kittyhawk III FR293		„
26 Oct		MC 202			„	„ „
27 Oct		MC 202			„	„ „
30 Oct		He 111 on ground	LG 21		„	„ „
„		Bf 109 on ground	„		„	„ „
„		Bf 109 Damaged on ground	„		„	„ „
31 Oct	2	Ju 87s			„	„ „
2 Nov	2	Ju 52s on ground	LG 21		„	„ „
„		Bf 109 on ground	„		„	„ „
5 Nov		Bf 109F			„	„ „
„		Bf 109F Damaged			„	„ „
12 Nov	2	Bf 109s on ground			„	„ „
„		Bf 109 Probable on ground			„	„ „
15 Nov		He 111			„	„ „
19 Nov		Bf 110			„	„ „
„		Bf 110 Damaged			„	„ „
11 Dec		Bf 109F			„	„ „
„		MC 202				FR213 „
13 Dec	1/2	Bf 109F			„	„ „
1943						
21 Jun	2	Bf 109s on ground	Comiso	in Spitfire V	BD-?	
7 Jul		MC 202	Comiso area	„	„	JK228

TOTAL: 23 and 3 shared destroyed, 2 unconfirmed destroyed (early 1940 classification), 4 and 1 shared probable, 5 and 1 shared damaged in air; 15 destroyed, 1 probably destroyed and 2 damaged on the ground.

(**NB** These totals compare with those which were written in my logbook in 1943, of 24 1/2 destroyed, 9 probables and 6 damaged, plus 13 destroyed on the ground. With the passing of time, and the fact that my logbook was frequently written up for me by other people within the various squadrons, this is as accurate as I can now get.)

* Although I recorded, on my return from hospital, that I had been shot down on 12 May 1940, and that my claims and service with 1 Squadron ended on that date, I now note from the squadron's own records that my final combats actually occurred one day later, on 13 May.

APPENDIX III

PERSONALITIES MENTIONED IN THE TEXT

Biographical Notes

Christopher Shores has been kind enough to supply brief biographical notes regarding most of the people I have mentioned while recounting my story. They are arranged here alphabetically. Further details of many of them can be found in other Grub Street books such as *Aces High, Aces High, Vol 2, Above the Trenches, Stars & Bars*, and the forthcoming *Those Other Eagles*, and where this is the case, this also is indicated, as are details of any autobiographies or biographies which have been written by, or about, any of them. I have not sought to include notes on the various national leaders who I have mentioned, nor of the main army commanders, all of whom are generally already well-known and recorded.

NB Please note that a number of the pilots who are identified in the captions to certain of the photographs, are not mentioned in the text. Notes on such personalities are not included in this section, but where names are marked *, details regarding them can be found in *Aces High* and/or *Aces High, Volume 2*. When marked ** such details may be found in *Those Other Eagles*, when published.

ANDERSON, Alan Ford, DFC, was a serving officer who had transferred to the RAF from the army. He took command of 613 Squadron in January 1940. He converted the unit from Hector biplanes to Lysanders in April, and in May/June led the unit in undertaking air supply to the surrounded defenders of Calais, for which he received a DFC. In December 1940, as a Wg Cdr, he commanded 268 Squadron, converting this unit from Lysanders to Curtiss Tomahawks during the spring of 1941. On 19 October he flew the first 'Rhubarb' sortie over the French coast in one of these aircraft. In 1942 he converted the unit to North American Mustang Is, leading it during the Dieppe operation of 19 August that year. During the early 1950s he was station commander at Linton-on-Ouse.

ATHERTON, Geoffrey Charles, DFC & Bar, was a Tasmanian who joined the RAAF early in the war. After brief service with a couple of squadrons flying Wirraways, he joined 75 RAAF Squadron, seeing considerable action over Port Moresby, New Guinea, during 1942, flying Curtiss Kittyhawks, and claiming a number of victories. In 1943 he was for a time a controller with 9 Fighter Sector, then commanding 82 RAAF Squadron. In 1944 he moved to 80 RAAF Squadron, but later in the year became Wing Leader of 78 RAAF Wing. He was shot down into the sea by AA fire during February 1945, but was successfully picked up. Late in the war he became Chief Instructor at 8 OTU in Australia, but in 1947 he transferred to the RAF on a Permanent Commission, serving with the Day Fighter Leaders' School at CFE, West Raynham. He has since died in his home town of Launceston, Tasmania. (See *Aces High* and *Aces High, Vol 2* for more details.)

BADER, Sir Douglas Robert Stewart, KBE, CBE, DSO & Bar, DFC & Bar, entered Cranwell in 1928, graduating in 1930 and joining 23 Squadron. A great sportsman, he played rugby for the RAF, Harlequins, Surrey and a Combined Services team, and also cricket for the RAF. On 14 December 1931 he crashed a Bulldog whilst low-flying, and had both legs amputated as a result. After recovery, he worked for Shell Petroleum until 1939, when he managed to get back into the RAF as a fighter pilot, despite his artificial limbs. He served briefly with 19 Squadron, then going to 222 Squadron as a flight commander, seeing action over Dunkirk. In July he was given command of the predominantly Canadian 242 Squadron, leading this unit and others from Duxford during the Battle of Britain. He became engaged in controversy when he pressed his AOC, Leigh-Mallory, to seek a greater role for his 'Big Wing' with Keith Park and Sir Hugh Dowding. He was awarded a DSO in October 1940, followed by a DFC in January 1941, a Bar to his DSO in July and a Bar to his DFC in September 1941. Meanwhile he had been appointed Wing Leader at Tangmere in March 1941. On 9 August 1941 he was heard to make claims for two Bf 109s, when he was believed to have collided with another and baled out. It is now believed that he had actually been shot down by another Messerschmitt. With his claims standing at 20 and four shared, six and one shared probables, he became a POW, first being entertained by the pilots of Jagdgeschwader 26. After several escape attempts he was imprisoned in Colditz Castle for the rest of the war. Released in 1945, he left the service in February 1946 and returned to Shell. Subsequently knighted, he became a national figure, doing much charity work to support and encourage other limbless people. His biography, *Reach for the Sky*, by Paul Brickhill (Collins, 1954) was made into a film, and a second biography was prepared by his brother-in-law, P.B. 'Laddie' Lucas. He died suddenly on 5 September 1982 after attending a dinner in honour of Air Chief Marshal Sir Arthur Harris. (See *Aces High* for more details.)

BARTHROPP, Patrick Peter Colum, DFC, an Irishman from Dublin, but educated in England, commenced work as an engineering apprentice with Rover cars. 'Paddy' joined the RAF on a short service commission in November 1938, becoming an Army Co-operation pilot. He volunteered for Fighter Command in August 1940, joining 602 Squadron in September. He moved to 610 Squadron, and then to 91 Squadron in February, where I first came to know him. He returned to 610 Squadron as a flight commander in August 1941, but then spent a period as an instructor before joining 122 Squadron in May 1942. Two days later he was shot down by an FW 190 and spent the rest of the war as a POW. He took part in the 'Great Escape' from Stalag Luft III, but was re-captured, and was one of the lucky ones who were not shot. After the war he attended the Empire Test Pilots School, then undertaking various postings until 1952 when he became Wing Commander Flying at Waterbeach, adding an AFC to his DFC. Here he got to lead one of the formations of Meteors during the Coronation Review Flypast in 1953. He was then posted to Hong Kong, returning to command a couple of smaller airfields. He left the service in 1957, setting up and running a high-class limousine service in West London with great success. He also wrote a small autobiography, *Paddy* (Howard Baker, 1987). (See *Aces High* and *Aces High, Vol 2* for more details.)

BARTLE, John Phillip, DFC, a native of Western Australia known as 'Jack', joined the RAAF in 1940 and served with 112 Squadron from September 1941, becoming a flight commander in May 1942 and acting briefly as temporary commanding officer pending my arrival. During this period he claimed five or six Axis aircraft shot down. After commanding 1 Air Ambulance Unit, he commenced a second tour as CO of 450 Squadron until November 1943. Posted to the UK, he was prepared for command of a Typhoon Wing, but after a few sorties was suddenly ordered back to Australia for staff duties. Here he became Chief Instructor of the School of Army Air Co-operation in Canberra. Towards the end of the war he transferred to the infantry as a major, subsequently becoming a successful businessman in timber, and later in livestock rearing. (See *Aces High* for more details.)

BEAMISH, Francis Victor, DSO & Bar, DFC, AFC, was born in County Cork, Eire, but lived in Ulster before entering the RAF College, Cranwell. He graduated in 1925, then serving in India with 31 and 60 Squadrons. In late 1926 he returned to the UK to undertake an instructors' course at CFS, then becoming an instructor at 5 FTS. In 1927 he joined the staff at Cranwell, whilst in 1931 he became a flight commander in 25 Squadron, on fighters for the first time. He then contracted tuberculosis and was retired from the service in October 1933, becoming a civil instructor at 2 FTS. By January 1937 his health had recovered enough for him to be reinstated, and late that year he became commanding officer of 64 Squadron, being awarded an AFC. After a spell at Staff College, he took over 504 Squadron in September 1939, but was sent on a special mission to Canada, January-June 1940. On return in early June he became airfield commander at North Weald, but flew on every possible occasion over France and England throughout the rest of the year. He was awarded a DSO and DFC. In March 1941 he was posted to HQ, 11 Group, but returned to North Weald later in the year, receiving a Bar to his DSO in September and promotion to Grp Capt. On 12 February 1942 he and his Wing Leader, Wg Cdr Finlay Boyd, spotted the German capital ships *Scharnhorst* and *Gneisenau* heading through the English Channel and raised the alarm. However, on 28 March 1942 he was leading the Wing over France when his Spitfire was seen to be damaged by a Bf 109. It disappeared into cloud, and was not seen again. At the time of his death he had claimed ten destroyed (one of them shared) and 11 probables (again, one shared). A biography, *Wings Aflame* by Doug Stokes (William Kimber) was published in 1985. (See *Aces High* and *Aces High, Vol 2* for more information.)

BERRY, Frederick George, DFM, joined the RAF as an Aircraft Apprentice in 1929. He was selected for pilot training in 1936, on conclusion of which he joined 43 Squadron at Tangmere as a Sgt. He was posted to 1 Squadron in August 1939, going to France with the unit where he was promoted Flt Sgt in April 1940. According to Paul Richey he claimed six victories there, the last of them an He 111 over St Nazaire on 17 June 1940 after it had bombed the troopship *Lancastrian*. He was awarded a DFM, but on 1 September 1940 was shot down and killed during the Battle of Britain. (See *Aces High* and *Aces High, Vol 2* for more details.)

BONG, Richard Ira, entered the USAAF in May 1941. After a short spell as an instructor he was posted to the 9th Fighter Squadron, 49th Fighter Group, equipped with Lockheed P-38 Lightning fighters. Accompanying the unit to Australia, he soon moved up to Port Moresby, New Guinea, where he commenced a highly successful fighting career. Having claimed 20 victories by November 1943, he was sent home on leave to the US. On his return he was given a freelance role with HQ, 5th Fighter Command, on 12 April 1944 passing Rickenbacker's World War I record of 26 victories. He was then again sent home to the US, not returning to New Guinea until October. He then raised his total to 40 by December to become the top-scoring US fighter pilot of the war. Awarded the Medal of Honor, DSO, Silver Star and numerous DFCs and Air Medals, he returned home for the third and last time at the end of December, but on 6 August 1945 when the jet Lockheed P-80 Shooting Star which he was flying, suffered a flame-out on take-off, he baled out too low and was killed. (See *Stars and Bars* for more details.)

BOUCHIER, Cecil Arthur, OBE, DFC, known as 'Boy', served as a Flg Off with the RAF contingent in North Russia in 1919, where he was awarded his DFC. As a Grp Capt he commanded RAF Hornchurch from December 1939 – December 1940, throughout the Battle of Britain. He was later promoted Air Commodore, and commanded the RAF component of the British Occupation Forces in Japan following the end of the war. He subsequently reached air rank.

BRAHAM, John Robert Daniel, DSO & 2 Bars, DFC & 2 Bars, joined the RAF in 1937 on a short service commission, where he became known as 'Bob'. He served with 29 Squadron from 1938, and as this unit was equipped with Bristol Blenheim Ifs, became a night fighter, claiming one of the earliest victories over England in this role. When the unit received Beaufighters, he was able to add six more victories during 1941. He then served as an instructor at 51 OTU, returning to 29 Squadron in 1942. By the end of that year he had added five more victories, one of them by day. He was then posted to 141 Squadron, where he undertook the first bomber support operations over Europe in Beaufighters equipped with the 'Serrate' device which homed on German night fighters' radar. In this role he was to add a further eight successes, including the shooting down of three of the Luftwaffe's leading night fighter pilots. After attending the Army Staff College at Camberley, he was appointed Wg Cdr Night Operations at HQ, 2 Group. In this role he frequently 'borrowed' Mosquitos from the Group's units, during the spring of 1944 claiming nine further victories during day 'Ranger' sorties, mainly around the Danish coast. This raised his total of claims to 29, 19 by night, but on 25 June 1944 he was intercepted and shot down, spending the rest of the war as a POW. After the war he formed the Night Fighter Development Wing at CFE, but in March 1946 left to join the colonial police. He rejoined three months later, receiving a permanent commission. Concerned by the poor pay in the RAF, he left in 1952 for Canada, where he joined the RCAF, serving until 1968. He then joined the Department of Historic Sites and Indian Affairs, but died on 7 February 1974 at the age of 53, due to an inoperable brain tumour. (See his autobiography, *Scramble* [Frederick Muller, 1961, and William Kimber, 1985], his biography, *Night Fighter Ace* by Tony Spooner, [Sutton Publishing, 1997], and *Aces High*, for more details.)

BROADHURST, Sir Harry, GCB, KBE, DSO, DFC & Bar, AFC, initially joined the Royal Artillery, but transferred to the RAF in 1926. He saw service in India on the North-West Frontier before returning to the UK in 1931 to become a fighter pilot. Subsequently he won the Brooke-Popham Trophy for air firing in three consecutive years. After service with 2 Group, Bomber Command, and attendance at the Staff College at Andover, he was given command of 111 Squadron in January 1939. A year later he became Station Commander at Coltishall, but in February 1940 was posted to 60 Wing in France. Following the withdrawal from that country, he commanded RAF Wittering, and then from December 1940, RAF Hornchurch, being promoted Grp Capt in June 1941. After a lecture tour in the USA, he became deputy SASO at 11 Group, Fighter Command, in May 1942. Still frequently leading squadrons over France, he had claimed 13 destroyed and seven probables by the late summer of that year. He then went out to the Middle East as SASOP, Western Desert Air Force. He became AOC in early 1943, becoming the youngest Air Vice-Marshal in the RAF at the age of 38. In early 1944 he returned to the UK to command 83 Group, 2nd Tactical Air Force, for the invasion of France. In 1945 he became Air Officer i/c Administration at Fighter Command, and then AOC, 61 Group, in 1947. A spell as SASO, 2nd TAF, led to him becoming C-in-C here in 1954. In 1956 he became AOC-in-C, Bomber Command, and an Air Chief Marshal. Highly decorated, he next became Commander, Allied Air Forces, Central Europe, until 1961, when he retired from the service to join A.V.Roe & Co Ltd as Managing Director. In 1965 he became Deputy Managing Director of Hawker Siddeley Aviation Ltd, of which A.V. Roe formed a part, and in 1968 a Director of the Group until his retirement in 1976. He died in retirement in Sussex in August 1995. (See *Aces High* and *Aces High, Vol 2*, for more details.)

BROOKER, Richard Edgar Peter, DSO & Bar, DFC & Bar, joined the RAF in July 1937, being posted to 56 Squadron in February 1938, and seeing action with this unit over southern England in summer 1940. He then became an instructor at the new CGS, Sutton Bridge, until April 1941, when he commanded 1 Squadron, being awarded a DFC. In January 1942 he was posted to Singapore, where he took command of 232 Squadron, claiming three victories against the Japanese before the fall of the East Indies, receiving a Bar to his DFC. Evacuated to Australia, he helped form and commanded 77 RAAF Squadron, but then returned to the UK. Here he joined SLAIS as an instructor, with promotion to Wg Cdr, whilst in May 1944 he became Wing Leader of 123 Wing on Typhoons. He was rested from July until January 1945, when, immediately after being awarded a DSO, he was posted as Wing Leader of 122 Wing on Tempests in Holland. He claimed his eighth victory with this unit, but on 16 April 1945 he was shot down and killed when in combat with FW 190Ds. The award of a Bar to his DSO was announced some time later. (See *Aces High* and *Aces High, Vol 2* for more details.)

BROTHERS, Peter Malam, DSO, DFC & Bar, joined the RAF in 1936 and was posted to 32 Squadron on conclusion of his training, becoming a flight commander in late 1938. He saw much action with this unit throughout the spring and summer of 1940, but moved to 257 Squadron in September. After a rest from operations, he formed and commanded 457 (RAAF) Squadron in June 1941. A year later he took command of 602 Squadron, while in October 1942 he became Wing Leader at Tangmere. Another spell as an OTU instructor followed until 1944, when he led first the Exeter and then the Culmhead Wings during the Normandy invasion. In October he attended the Fort Leavenworth General Staff School in the USA with myself, then serving at CFE until March 1947 when he left the RAF to join the colonial service in Kenya. He rejoined the RAF in 1949, commanding 57(B) Squadron on Avro Lincolns and then Boeing Washington (B-29) heavy bombers until 1952. In 1955 he returned to Fighter Command, but then in 1957 served at RAF Marham V-bomber airfield. As a Grp Capt he was a Staff Officer at SHAPE, 1959-62, then Director of Operations (Overseas), 1962-65. As an Air Cdr he was AOC, Military Air Traffic Operations, 1966-68, and then Director of Public Relations (RAF) until 1973. Awarded a CBE in 1964, he now lives in retirement in Berkshire. (See *Aces High* and *Aces High, Vol 2*, for more details.)

BROWN, George Alfred, DFC, was a career officer who joined the RAF in 1937. He was wounded during the Battle of Britain whilst serving with 253 Squadron, but on recovery became a flight commander in the first 'Eagle' Squadron (No. 71) formed of US volunteers. In August 1941 he commanded 133, the third 'Eagle' Squadron. After a spell at HQ, Fighter Command, he became CFI at 55 OTU, Annan, before being sent out to the Middle East, where he remained for the rest of the war. He retired from the RAF as a Grp Capt in July 1962 and thereafter became much involved with the Air Training Corps in Wales, becoming local Commandant for ten years until 1977. He died in 1998. (See *Those Other Eagles* for more details.)

BROWN, Mark Henry, DFC & Bar, from Manitoba, Canada, joined the RAF in May 1936 and was posted to 1 Squadron. He saw action with the unit throughout the first year of the war, becoming a flight commander in late May 1940, and then commanding officer in November. In May 1941 he was posted to an OTU as an instructor, and in July was promoted Wg Cdr. He went out to Malta in November 1941, becoming Wing Leader at Takali on the 5th. Just one week later he was shot down and killed by ground fire while leading a strafing attack on Gela airfield, Sicily. By this time he had claimed 15 and four shared shot down. (See *Wings of the Morning* by his sister, Jean Brown Segal [The MacMillan Coy. of Canada], *Aces High* and *Aces High, Vol 2*, for more details.)

BRYAN, John Michael, DFC & Bar, joined the RAFVR during 1940. He completed his training in Canada, and was commissioned during 1941. He then served with 137 Squadron on Whirlwinds, and later on Hurricane IVs, during 1942-3, becoming a flight commander. In August 1943 he was posted to command 198 Squadron on Typhoons, concluding his tour in November. He returned to the unit in April 1944, but the following month was appointed Wing Leader, 136 Wing. He was shot down by flak and killed on 10 June 1944. (See *Aces High*, and *Aces High, Vol 2*, for more details.)

BURTON, Howard Frizelle, DSO, DFC & Bar, graduated from the RAF College, Cranwell, as winner of the Sword of Honour, at the end of 1936. He was posted to 46

Squadron, and from there in October 1939 to 66 Squadron as a flight commander. He saw action over Dunkirk and during the Battle of Britain, in September 1940 being given command of 616 Squadron. He was to lead this unit for a year, much of that time as part of Douglas Bader's Tangmere Wing. In early 1942 he was posted to the Middle East where he became Wing Leader of 239 Wing. With the end of the Tunisian Campaign in May 1943, he had claimed two and four shared victories, and was then sent home on leave to England in General Montgomery's personal aircraft. Returning in a Hudson with a number of other senior officers on 3 June 1943, the aircraft was intercepted over the Bay of Biscay by a Luftwaffe long-range fighter and was shot down with the loss of all aboard, which included Sqn Ldr O.V. Hanbury, commanding officer of 260 Squadron. (See *Aces High* and *Aces High Volume 2*, for more details.)

CALDWELL, Clive Robertson, DSO, DFC & Bar, from Sydney, Australia, had obtained a private pilot's licence before the war and joined the RAAF on the outbreak. He was posted to the Middle East in May 1941, where he joined 250 Squadron which was just taking the first Curtiss Tomahawks into action. Over the next few months he enjoyed considerable success, and gained the nickname 'Killer'; on one occasion he was even able to claim five Ju 87 Stuka dive bombers in a single action. By the end of the year he had been credited with 12 and one shared destroyed. He was then posted to command 112 Squadron, and whilst much involved in testing the unit's new Kittyhawks for the bomb-carrying role, he nonetheless managed to add a further five victories by May 1942. He was then sent home to Australia at the request of his government, but travelled via England, where he gained some experience in flying Spitfires. On arrival in Australia, he served briefly with 2 OTU, then becoming Wing Leader of 1 Fighter Wing at Darwin with the first Spitfires in the Far East. Here he was to claim seven victories against the Japanese during 1943, before spending a further spell at 2 OTU as CFI. In May 1945 he took command of 80 Wing as a Grp Capt, but little opposition was to be found in the air, despite a move to Morotai Island. Feeling that the Americans were now leaving the RAAF out of the serious fighting, he and a number of other senior officers protested vociferously. He was then court martialled for reputedly dealing in alcohol with US personnel and was reduced in rank to Flt Lt. He appealed against this, and in February 1946 left the service. He then went into business very successfully, until his death on 5 August 1994. (See *Aces High* and *Aces High, Vol 2*, for more details.)

CAREY, Frank Reginald, CBE, DFC & 2 Bars, AFC, DFM, was a South London lad who became an apprentice at RAF Halton at the age of 15. He then served as a metal rigger with 43 Squadron during the early 1930s, and then with various bomber squadrons. He was selected for pilot training in 1935, and like me, undertook this at 6 FTS, Netheravon. He rejoined 43 Squadron at Tangmere as a Sgt Pilot in September 1936, and after the outbreak of war achieved some early successes, receiving one of the first DFMs of the war. He was commissioned in April 1940 and was posted to 3 Squadron, seeing action in France with this unit during May. He was shot down and it was some time before he rejoined the unit, now back in England, where he found he had been posted as 'Missing', but had also been awarded the DFC and Bar. He then rejoined 43 Squadron, seeing considerable action during the Battle of Britain. In February 1941 he became an instructor, but in July joined 245 Squadron as a flight commander. A month later he formed and commanded 135 Squadron, leading this unit overseas in November – it was believed destined for the South Russian front. With the Japanese entry into the war, the unit was diverted to Burma, where he was to claim more successes. In February 1942 he was promoted Wing Leader of 267 Wing, and was awarded a Second Bar to his DFC. A year later he formed an Air Fighting Training Unit at Amarda Road which had great succcess in training both RAF and USAAF units. He moved to Egypt in November 1944 to command 73 OTU as a Grp Capt, receiving an AFC. Granted a permanent commission after the war, he led 135 Wing in Germany, flying Tempest IIs. He was later Wg Cdr Flying at Gutersloh on jets, various staff appointments following until 1958, when he became Air Adviser to the British High Commissioner in Australia. He retired from the RAF in June 1960, being made a CBE, and then became representative for Rolls-Royce Aero Division in Australia. One of the most successful RAF fighter pilots of the war, he claimed at least 25 and 3 shared, plus 4 more unconfirmed destroyed. (See *Aces High* for more details.)

CARSON, Kenneth F., from Queensland, Australia, served with 112 Squadron in the Western Desert during 1941-2. Initially a Sgt when he joined the unit, he was commissioned in April 1942. On 9 January 1942 he was forced down by a Bf 109, but returned safely to the unit on foot. On 16 June 1942 he was again brought down, this time by flak, and became a POW for the duration of the war (he was not killed, as his brother and I thought at the time). He had by this time claimed two aircraft shot down and a third shared. (See *Those Other Eagles* for more details.)

CARTER, Guy L., had already seen long service with the RAF when he became a flight commander at 5 FTS, Sealand, in 1935. During World War II he was posted to North Africa, where during 1941-2 he commanded first 258 Wing in 211 Group, and then 211 Group itself. Later in the war, whilst he was SASO of Desert Air Force, he was flying into Yugoslavia as a passenger in a Dakota, when the rather inexperienced pilot had trouble landing and had to go round again. This manoeuvre was undertaken rather coarsely, and in consequence a heavy box of tools broke loose and crashed into Carter's chest, killing him.

CASTELAIN, Noel, was born in Niort, France, in 1917. He volunteered for the Armée de l'Air in 1936, entering junior officers' school in June 1939 and gaining his wings at the end of that year. France fell before he completed training as a fighter pilot, but he fled to England where he attended 6 OTU. He was then despatched with several others to Dakar, but when the operation designed to occupy this French outpost failed, he was posted instead to Egypt, where he joined Free French Flight 1. Attached to 73 Squadron, he made his first shared claim during the defence of Tobruk. In October 1942 he volunteered for service with the French Groupe 'Normandie' forming in the Soviet Union, and flying Yak fighters with this unit on the Eastern Front, claimed six more victories before being shot down and killed on 16 July 1943. (See *Aces High, Vol 2* for more details.)

CLISBY, Leslie Redford, DFC, was an Australian from South Australia. He joined the RAAF as an officer cadet in 1935, and was granted a permanent commission in

1937. However, he then travelled to England to take up a short service commission in the RAF, and was posted to 1 Squadron. During the opening days of the German 'Blitzkrieg' of May 1940, he claimed about eight and three shared enemy aircraft destroyed, but on 15 May during a combat with some Bf 110s, he was shot down and killed. The award to him of a DFC effectively posthumously, created a considerable amount of controversy at the time, in which even His Majesty, King George VI, was involved. (See *Aces High* and *Aces High, Vol 2* for more details.)

CLOWES, Arthur Victor, DFM, known as 'Darky', was from Derbyshire. He had joined the RAF as a Boy Apprentice at Halton in 1929, and later obtained flying training, becoming a Sgt Pilot in 1 Squadron by 1939. He was one of only two pilots to remain with the unit throughout the 1940 fighting, in France and over England. He was commissioned in September, becoming a flight commander the following month. He was rested in April 1941, returning to operations in December as commanding officer of 79 Squadron. In early 1942 he was posted to the Middle East, where he later commanded 601 Squadron from August-November. He was then again rested until June 1943, when he took command of 94 Squadron. An accident in the Mess in September caused the loss of sight in one of his eyes and put an end to flying for him. He was granted a permanent commission in the Secretarial Branch after the war, but died of liver cancer on 7 December 1949. During his time as a fighter pilot he had claimed ten and one shared destroyed, one shared unconfirmed, and three probables. (See *Aces High* and *Aces High, Vol 2* for more details.)

CONINGHAM, Sir Arthur, DSO, MC, DFC, was born in Australia but lived in New Zealand. He served with the NZ Expeditionary Force in Samoa and Egypt, but was invalided out with typhoid in 1916. He then travelled to England and joined the RFC, during 1917 serving in France with 32 Squadron, flying DH 2s and DH 5s, becoming a flight commander. He became the top-scoring pilot on the latter type of aircraft, claiming nine victories during July of that year; he was awarded a DSO and MC. In 1918 he commanded 92 Squadron on SE 5as, claiming a further five victories to raise his total for the war to 14, and receiving a DFC. He was twice wounded in action whilst during these years. He remained in the RAF after 1918, his nickname of 'Maori' gradually being degraded to 'Mary'. In 1922 he was posted to Iraq, serving with 55 Squadron, of which he became commanding officer. Two years of staff work in Egypt followed, and then he returned to England in 1926 to become a senior instructor at the RAF College, Cranwell. In 1930 he was second in command of the Central Flying School, but he was then sent to the Sudan for three years as senior airman there. On return to the UK in 1935 he was posted to HQ, Coastal Area, while two years later he was promoted Grp Capt as SASO, 17 Group. In July 1939 he took command of 4 Group, Bomber Command, and then in July 1941 was posted to Egypt to command Western Desert Air Force. With the formation of North West African Tactical Air Forces in early 1943, he became AOC, remaining in command until brought back to the UK at the start of 1944 to command the new 2nd TAF. Now an Air Marshal, and knighted, following the end of the war he was appointed head of flying training, but was retired in 1947. On 30 January 1948, he took off for Bermuda in a British South American Airways Avro Tudor, Star Tiger. The aircraft never arrived. (See *Coningham; a Biography of Air Marshal Sir Arthur Coningham* by

Vincent Orange [Methuen, 1990] and *Above the Trenches* for more details.)

CONWAY, Alfred Gordon, DFC, was from North London. Born in 1923, he 'back-dated' his birth certificate by a year to allow him to join the RAFVR in November 1940. After training he was posted to 136 Squadron in October 1941, accompanying this unit out to the Far East soon after this date. Here he was to fly Hurricanes and then Spitfires against the Japanese, becoming one of the top scorers here with seven destroyed and one probable. After a spell off operations from March 1944 – May 1945, he took command of 155 Squadron. Returning to the UK in December 1945, he remained in the service, flying Meteors with 222 Squadron, 63 Squadron (as a flight commander) and then 92 Squadron as commanding officer, until May 1952. After attending Staff College, he became Wg Cdr Flying at Horsham St.Faith, 1953-6, whilst in 1961 he was Wg Cdr Operations at Gutersloh, Germany, on Hunters until 1964. He retired from the service in 1976, and lives in Suffolk. (See *Aces High* for more details.)

COX, Graham James, DFC & Bar, joined the RAF in 1930 as ground crew, subsequently receiving a short service commission in 1939. He saw action over England with 152 Squadron during 1940, ending his first tour in 1941. He commenced his second in September 1942 as a flight commander in 501 Squadron, but in May 1943 was posted to Tunisia where he took up a similar position in 43 Squadron. In July he became commanding officer of 229 Squadron on Malta. He undertook a third tour with 92 Squadron in Italy from February 1944, ending the war with eight and three shared victories to his credit. He left the RAF in 1946 and later went to Canada. Here he was killed in a flying accident in a Cessna light aircraft when in bad weather conditions over the country's Northern Territories. (See *Aces High* and *Aces High, Vol 2* for more details.)

CRAWFORD-COMPTON, William Vernon, DSO & Bar, DFC & Bar, from Invercargill, New Zealand, worked his way to the UK as a ship's carpenter in order to join the RAF when he arrived in September 1939. On completion of training he served initially as a Sgt in 603 Squadron, joining that unit in early 1941. He was commissioned in May and posted to 485 (RNZAF) Squadron, where by the end of April 1942 he had claimed six and one shared enemy aircraft. In August 1942 he joined 611 Squadron as a flight commander, whilst in December he was given command of 64 Squadron, which he led until March 1943. He then undertook staff work until June, when he was appointed Wing Leader at Hornchurch. He then led many escort sorties to US heavy bombers until October, when he left to undertake a lecture tour in the US. In April 1944 he returned to lead 145 Wing, 2nd TAF, remaining with this unit until early 1945. With at least 20 and one shared victories to his credit, he was awarded a permanent commission after the war. Service in the Mediterranean area was followed by a stint as Air Attaché to Norway in 1950, while in 1954 he commanded RAF Bruggen in Germany – a Sabre base. He was created a CBE in 1957 and a CB in 1965, and in 1967 he reached the rank of Air Vice-Marshal. At this time he was also Captain of the RAF ski team. His second marriage was to the mother of British Olympic gold medal swimmer, Duncan Goodhew. Bill Crawford-Compton died on 2 January 1988, aged 72. (See *Aces High* and *Aces High, Vol 2* for more details.)

CUKR, Vaclav, had escaped from Czechoslovakia to France, where he served as a Sergeant Chef with Groupe II/3 of the Armée de l'Air. During the fighting of May – June 1940, flying one of the latest Dewoitine 520 fighters, he was credited with two individual and four shared victories. Although converted onto Hurricanes in the UK, he did not then serve with any fighter units thereafter.

DAVID, William Dennis, DFC & Bar, a Londoner from Surbiton, Surrey, joined the RAFVR in 1937 and was granted a short service commission in February 1938. In early 1939 he joined 87 Squadron, going to France with this unit at the start of the war. During May 1940 he became one of the RAF's most successful pilots during the German 'Blitzkrieg', being awarded both DFC & Bar for at least 11 victories. He was to claim a further seven over south-west England during the summer and autumn, the last of these with 213 Squadron, to which he moved as a flight commander in September. In late 1940 he moved to 152 Squadron, but in March 1941 was rested with a spell as an instructor. He remained on such duties until the start of 1943, when he was posted to the Middle East as SASO, 209 Group. In July 1943 he took command of 89 Squadron, a night fighter unit, accompanying this to Ceylon later in the year. He saw service in this theatre for the rest of the war, being promoted Grp Capt, and becoming SASO, 224 Group, during 1945. With the end of the Far Eastern war, he accompanied the force sent to Java for operations against the nationalist insurgents there. Remaining in the RAF, he became Air Attaché in Hungary during the 1950s, where he assisted many in escaping to the West during the 1956 uprising. Awarded a CBE in 1967 when he retired from the RAF, he subsequently undertook much work for charity. He died suddenly on 25 August 2000, shortly after the publication of his autobiography. (See *Dennis 'Hurricane' David; My Autobiography* [Grub Street, 2000], *Aces High* and *Aces High, Vol 2* for more details.)

DeBOURKE, Richard, was a US citizen who joined the RCAF, and who flew with 112 Squadron in North Africa. He claimed three victories and a probable during late 1942, but on 10 March 1943 his was one of six Kittyhawks shot down by Luftwaffe fighters from Jagdgeschwader 77 over Tunisia, and he failed to survive. (See *Those Other Eagles* for more details.)

DEERE, Alan Christopher, DSO, OBE, DFC & Bar, DFC (US), was born and raised in New Zealand, but travelled to England in September 1937 to take up a short service commission in the RAF. He joined 54 Squadron in August 1938, and was with that unit at the outbreak of war, seeing considerable fighting over Dunkirk in May 1940. By the end of that month he had claimed nine victories (including one shared and one unconfirmed) and was awarded a DFC. During the summer he continued to achieve comparable success, but on 31 August his was one of three Spitfires caught by bombs whilst taking off from Hornchurch; all were destroyed, but all three pilots survived relatively unscathed. By this time he had claimed six more confirmed victories, one and one shared unconfirmed, and three probables, and he received a Bar to his DFC as the unit was rested. After a spell on controller duties, he joined 602 Squadron as a flight commander in May 1941, becoming CO in August. In January

1942 he was sent to the USA on a lecture tour, on return a month later, taking command of 403 (RCAF) Squadron. In August 1942 he went to HQ, 13 Group, on staff duties, but in February 1943 he joined 611 Squadron as a supernumary, then becoming Wing Leader at Biggin Hill. Awarded a DSO in July, he led the Wing until September 1943, when he was taken ill. His final claims during this period brought his total to at least 17 and one shared destroyed, two and one shared unconfirmed destroyed, and four probables. On recovery he commanded the Fighter Wing at CGS until March 1944, then joining the staff of 11 Group. In May he became Wing Leader of 145(French) Wing, which he led during the Normandy invasion. He then fulfilled a number of staff and command roles, including spending a year at the US Air University in 1946. As a Grp Capt he was Aide de Camp to HM the Queen, 1961-63, and in 1964 was promoted Air Commodore. He ended his service as Commandant of the Halton Apprentice School, retiring in 1967. He then worked as a civil servant at the Air Ministry. His autobiography, *Nine Lives* (Hodder & Stoughton, 1959) was subsequently re-published by Wingham Press. He died in September 1995, his ashes being sprinkled on the water of the Thames estuary from a Spitfire. (See *Aces High* and *Aces High, Vol 2* for more details.)

DEMOZAY, Jean-Francois, DSO, DFC & Bar, a Frenchman from Nantes, was called up in 1938, but was at once invalided out of the service. A civil pilot, he offered his services in September 1939, and was accepted for non-combatant duties, being attached to 1 Squadron, RAF, as an interpreter. In June 1940 he flew an abandoned Bristol Bombay transport to England, carrying 15 troops aboard. Here he joined the Free French, claiming to have been a fighter pilot, and using the *nom-de-guerre* Moses Morlaix, he was posted to 1 Squadron later in the year. Here he became a flight commander, claiming quite a lot of success. In June 1941 he was posted to 242 Squadron, and from there to 91 Squadron. In early 1942 he was rested, but returned to 91 Squadron in June, serving until the end of the year, by which time he had claimed 18 victories and two probables. Promoted Wg Cdr, he joined HQ, 11 Group, but in 1943 he was sent out to North Africa to set up a flying school for Free French pilots there. Returning to London in April 1944, he later led a Free French Groupe, attacking bypassed German garrisons along the French Atlantic coast. At the end of the war he was appointed deputy commander of all flying training schools in France, but on 19 December 1945 he crashed during a flight to London, and was killed. He was awarded French and Belgian Croixes de Guerre, the US DFC and the Czech War Cross. (See *Aces High* for more details.)

DENIS, James, DFC, another Frenchman, joined the Armée de l'Air in 1929 as a Sgt, becoming a fighter pilot. He served with the 3 Regiment de Chasse from 1930-36, and by the time of the French Armistice in June 1940 was already 33 years old. He escaped to England in a Farman 222 on 20 June, joining the Free French as a Sous Lt, to become an instructor. In August 1940 he was sent with a group of other pilots to Dakar, where a Free French take-over was hoped for. When this failed, his group were flown across Africa to Egypt, where he joined Free French Flight 1. After attachments to several British units, the Flight operated from within the besieged port of Tobruk as part of 73 Squadron, where in 24 days he claimed six and one shared victories. The following year, promoted Capitaine, he was a flight commander in the new Groupe de Chasse 'Alsace', but health problems ended his operational flying, and he joined the Free French HQ in Beirut. After the war he enjoyed a long and distinguished career in the Armée de l'Air, dying in retirement during the 1990s. (See *Aces High*, and *Aces High, Vol 2* for more details.)

DICKINSON, E., joined the RAFVR during 1941 and on completion of training was commissioned and posted to the Middle East. He joined 112 Squadron in December of that year, subsequently claiming one confirmed and one damaged during the Operation 'Crusader' fighting. He was promoted to command a flight; on 27 May 1942 he was shot down, but returned on foot next day. He flew a further sortie at once, but from this one he failed to return, his body never being found. It is believed that he had been shot down in flames by Bf 109s of II/JG 27.

DONALDSON, Edward Mortlock, DSO, from Dorset, was one of three brothers who all became notable fighter pilots with the RAF. Joining the service in 1934, he first served with 54 Squadron. He then became an instructor during 1939-40, before becoming commanding officer of 263 Squadron on Whirlwind twin-engined fighters during 1941. In August 1942 he was posted to Malta to become Wing Leader at Takali. Here he was shot down and badly wounded on 14 October, losing two fingers from his left hand. Flown out in a Liberator at the start of November, he was one of those to survive when it crashed into the sea whilst attempting to land at Gibraltar. He remained in the RAF, becoming commanding officer at Biggin Hill, 1950-51, and SASO, 2 Group, 2nd TAF, 1953-56. He retired in March 1959 and died on 5 October 1980. (See *Aces High* and *Aces High, Vol 2* for more details.)

DONNET, Michael Gabriel Libert Marie, DFC, a Belgian, although born in England, was an officer cadet in the Belgian air service in 1939. He saw action during May 1940 as a reconnaissance pilot, flying Renard R 31s, then being taken to Germany as a POW. He was later released and returned home, obtaining work. He and several friends discovered that a Stampe SV 4 aircraft was locked in a hangar in the grounds of a chateau which was in use by the German army as a mess. In great secrecy they worked by night on this aircraft until it was ready to fly, Donnet and L.Divoy, another pilot, then taking off and flying to England in July 1941. Here he was accepted into the RAF and in November joined 64 Squadron, becoming a flight commander in 1942, receiving a DFC, and becoming commanding officer in March 1943. In November 1943 he became an instructor at the FLS, then at Aston Down, and at Milfield from February. In March 1944 he commanded 350 Squadron, then becoming Wing Leader at Hawkinge. In February 1945 he led the Bentwaters Mustang Wing, leading the fighter escort to the attack on the Gestapo HQ in Copenhagen. After the war he served initially at the Belgian Minstry of Defence as head of the Belgian Fighter Force. He then became SASO of 83 (Anglo-Belgian) Group in 2nd TAF, before holding a number of staff appointments, ultimately Chairman of the NADGE Policy Board of NATO and Belgian Military Representative of the NATO Military Committee. He retired as Lt Gen Aviateur Baron Michael Donnet, CVO, DFC, C de G (Belge), FRAeS. (See *Flight to Freedom* by Michael Donnet, Ian Allan Ltd, 1974, and Wingham Press Ltd, 1991, and *Those Other Eagles* for more details.)

DOUGLAS, Sir William Sholto, KCB, MC, DFC, was one of the earliest pilots of the RFC. During 1915 he served with 8 Squadron, flying BE 2s, but in April 1916 he formed and commanded 43 Squadron on Sopwith 1½ Strutters, being awarded an MC. In May 1917 he was rested, returning to France in August to lead 84 Squadron, which was equipped with SE 5As. He was to lead this unit until the end of the war, claiming one victory personally during October 1918. He was promoted Acting Lt Col, and was awarded a DFC shortly after the close of hostilities. After a very successful career between the wars, he was an Air Vice-Marshal and Deputy Chief of Air Staff in 1939. Promoted Air Marshal, he took over as AOC-in-C of Fighter Command from Sir Hugh Dowding in late November 1940, remaining at the helm for two years. In January 1943, with further promotion to Air Chief Marshal, he replaced Tedder as AOC, Middle East Command when the latter became Air Commander-in-Chief, Mediterranean Air Command. A year later he handed over to Sir Keith Park and returned to England to head Coastal Command, which he did until the end of June 1945. He then took up the role of Air C-in-C, British Air Forces of Occupation, in Germany. He was later ennobled as Marshal of the Royal Air Force Lord Douglas of Kirtleside, GCB, MC, DFC.

DUKE, Neville Frederick, DSO, DFC & 2 Bars, from Tonbridge, Kent, joined the RAFVR in June 1940, and in February 1941 was posted to 92 Squadron. In October he was sent to the Middle East where he served initially with 112 Squadron, flying Tomahawks, and later, Kittyhawks. By February 1942 he had claimed eight and three probables, but his tour ended in April, just before I took over the unit. After a period as an instructor, in November he rejoined 92 Squadron, now also in North Africa, where he became a flight commander during January 1943. His second tour ended in June, by which time he had added claims for 14 more enemy aircraft shot down. He then became an instructor again until March 1944, when he commenced his third tour as commanding officer of 145 Squadron. Here he claimed five more victories to achieve a total of 26 and two shared, making him Allied Mediterranean top scorer. In October 1944 he returned to the UK where he became a production test pilot with Hawker Aircraft. One year later he attended the Fourth Course at the Empire Test Pilots' School at Cranfield, then being posted to the RAF High Speed Flight in 1946. A spell at the A & AEE, Boscombe Down, followed, and he was awarded an AFC in 1948. He left the service that year to join Hawkers as a test pilot, becoming Chief Test Pilot in 1951. He tested all Hawker's early jets up to and including the Hunter, and on 7 September 1953 gained the World Air Speed Record at 727.65 mph in a special all-red Hunter (WB188); he was awarded an OBE that year. In August 1955 he crash-landed a Hunter on Thorney Island after a gun-firing problem and damaged his back. On 9 May 1956 he suffered more damage to his back in a crash in the P.1099 prototype as a result of which he was obliged to retire that October, having received the Queen's Commendation for Valuable Service in the Air. He then followed a career of freelance flying and consultancy work until his retirement. He now lives in Hampshire, still on occasion flying his own aircraft. (See *Test Pilot* [Allan Wingate, 1953, and Grub Street, 1992], *The War Diaries of Neville Duke, 1941-1944* edited by Norman Franks, Grub Street, 1995, *Aces High* and *Aces High, Vol 2* for more details.)

EDWARDES-JONES, (John) Sir Humphrey, KCB, CBE, DFC, AFC, BA, known as E.J. in the RAF, was a serving officer between the wars. In May 1937 he was posted from A&AEE, where he had been testing the prototype Spitfire, to command 213 Squadron on the latter's re-formation. He led the unit aggressively during the Dunkirk evacuation, but on 7 June 1940 was posted to command 6 OTU, Sutton Bridge, as a Wg Cdr. In late 1942, now a Grp Capt, he commanded 323 Wing during the invasion of French North-West Africa, with Michael Pedley as his Wg Cdr Flying. He enjoyed a long and successful career in the RAF postwar, becoming SASO, and then AOC-in-C, RAF Germany, as an Air Marshal during the late 1950s.

EISENHOWER, Dwight David, led a relatively unspectacular career in the US Army between the wars. It was something of a surprise when he was appointed Allied Supreme Commander for the invasion of French North-West Africa in late 1942. During that campaign his future was at times precarious when US forces suffered early setbacks. However, during 1943 his diplomatic skills in co-ordinating the efforts of his diverse forces in the Mediterranean area became more obvious, and he successfully presided over the victory in North Africa, and the invasions of Sicily and Italy. Called to the UK at the start of 1944 as Allied supremo for the invasion of Normandy, he retained his position throughout the rest of the war, generally with great success. Subsequently he became President of the United States during the 1950s.

ELLIS, John, DFC & Bar, from Deal, Kent, joined the RAF in March 1936. Serving with 213 Squadron at the outbreak of war, he was posted to 610 Squadron of the Auxiliary Air Force as a flight commander, seeing action over Dunkirk. He became commanding officer in July 1940, and by the end of the year had claimed 12 and two shared victories, adding one more by night in March 1941. He then became an instructor and was posted to the Middle East as Wg Cdr Flying at 71 OTU in the Sudan. In spring 1943 he was posted to Malta to lead the Krendi Wing, but on 13 June was shot down over Sicily, becoming a POW; his place was then taken by myself. After the war he became Wg Cdr Training at HQ, Fighter Command, later commanding RAF Molesworth and then RAF Bentwaters. A spell as o/c Flying at Horsham St Faith followed, and then the Staff College. After serving at the Air Ministry, he went back to the Middle East for a spell, returning to command the Admin Wing at Tangmere. Promoted Grp Capt in 1959, he received the OBE in 1956 and CBE in 1960. He retired from the service in 1967 and died during 2001. (See *Aces High* and *Aces High, Vol 2* for more details.)

EMBRY, Sir Basil, DSO & two Bars, DFC, AFC, was commissioned in the RAF in 1921. He served initially in Iraq with 45 and then 30 Squadron, returning to the UK in 1927 to become an instructor. He then served in India with 1 Indian Wing on the North-West Frontier, being promoted Wg Cdr during 1938 when he also received his first award of the DSO. Back in the UK in 1939, he commanded 21 Squadron and then 107 Squadron, both equipped with Bristol Blenheim IV bombers, undertaking many dangerous daylight raids over France and Norway. When about to be promoted Grp Capt, he was shot down over France on 26 May 1940 and was captured, but managed to escape and make his way back to the UK via Spain. (See *Wingless Victory* by Arthur Richardson; Oldham Press, 1950.) After a long leave he became SASO 6

Group, but offered to command a night fighter unit at Rochester; however this was disbanded in December 1940 and he became station commander at Wittering, often taking part in operational flights. In late 1941 he was posted to Western Desert Air Force as an adviser, returning in March 1942. In 1943 he became SASO, 10 Group, but in May took command of 2 Group, Bomber Command, which was then transferred to 2nd TAF control. Now an Air Vice-Marshal, he continued to fly operations as 'Wg Cdr Smith', taking part in the attacks on SS barracks at Egleton in August 1944 and on Gestapo headquarters in Aarhus and Odense in October 1944 and April 1945. As a CB and KBE, he then became Director-General of Training until April 1949, when he was appointed AOC-in-C, Fighter Command. In July 1953 he became C-in-C, Allied Air Forces Central Europe. Frustrated by the NATO organisation, he spoke bluntly about its need for reorganisation, and in consequence was prematurely retired from the RAF in February 1956.

FAJTL, Frantisek, DFC, served with the Czech Air Force from 1933 as a bomber pilot. In May 1939 he escaped to France via Poland, where he was subsequently trained as a fighter pilot. He made his way to England after the fall of France, and was commissioned in the RAF. He was posted briefly to 310 (Czech) and 1 Squadrons, then joining 17 Squadron in September 1940, where he claimed his first victories. In May 1941 he was posted to 313(Czech) Squadron, becoming a flight commander in December. In April 1942 he was given command of 122 Squadron, but on 5 May he was shot down by an FW 190, crash-landing in France. He evaded capture, making his way back to England via Spain and Gibraltar, arriving in August 1942. He then undertook staff duties until September 1943, when he retured to 313 Squadron as CO. In February 1944 he went to the Soviet Union to join the Czech fighter unit being formed there, commanding the 128th Fighter Squadron on the Eastern Front for the rest of the war. He then commanded the 1st Fighter Regiment in the new Czech Air Force until the Communist coup in February 1948, when he was arrested and dismissed. He was reinstated in 1990 as a General Major, living in retirement in Prague. (See *Those Other Eagles* for more details.)

FELL, Michael Frampton, DSC & Bar, was a very illustrious officer of the Fleet Air Arm. In 1940 he flew Skuas as a Sub Lt with 800 Squadron, seeing action from the deck of HMS *Ark Royal* during the opening months of the war with Italy in the Mediterranean. He later served land-based in North Africa with the RN Fighter Squadron, making claims whilst flying both Hurricanes and Martlets. He remained with 805 Squadron on the latter aircraft until January 1943, having claimed four shared victories and a probable since 1940. Promoted rapidly, he commanded 878 Squadron, again on Martlets, until October 1943, taking part in the invasions of Sicily and Salerno. He then became Wing Leader of 7 Naval Fighter Wing until December 1944. During this period he took part in strikes on the German battleship *Tirpitz* in Trondheim Fjord; in the invasion of southern France in August 1944, and in a sweep through the Aegean thereafter. For these actions he was awarded a DSO and DSC, and twice Mentioned in Despatches. After the war he received a Bar to his DSC in 1952 for operations over Korea when Commander Air on HMAS *Sydney*. In January 1969, now a Rear Admiral, he became a CB as Flag Officer, Carriers and Amphibious Ships. He has since died. (See *Those Other Eagles* for more details.)

GARTON, Geoffrey William, DSO, DFC, joined the RAF in May 1937. Posted initially to 43 Squadron at Tangmere in early 1940, he then joined 73 Squadron in France in May. Following the fighting there and over England during the summer, he accompanied the unit to Africa. Ending his first tour in April 1941, he was commissioned and became a test pilot. He returned to operations a year later with 250 Squadron on Kittyhawks. From there he was posted to 112 Squadron as a flight commander on 21 June 1942, receiving the award of a DFC at that time. He became commanding officer in January 1943 following my departure. He was rested again in May, but at the end of 1943 commenced a third tour at the head of 232 Squadron. He was injured in a car accident in Italy in April 1944, and was off flying for several months. In August he took over 87 Squadron in 8 SAAF Wing, whilst in April 1945 he became Wing Leader of that wing. At the end of the war he resumed command of 87, and was awarded a DSO. By that time he had claimed seven and three shared victories. He remained in the RAF until February 1962, retiring as a Wg Cdr. He died in November 1976. (See *Aces High* and *Aces High, Vol 2* for more details.)

GIBBES, Robert Henry Maxwell, DSO, DFC & Bar, from Manley, New South Wales, joined 450 Squadron on its formation in February 1941, accompanying it to Egypt, where he transferred to 3 RAAF Squadron. He saw action over Syria against the Vichy French, and then in the Desert. Here he became commanding officer in February 1942. He was shot down by the gunner in a Ju 88 on 26 May 1942, baling out and breaking his ankle. He soon returned to action, flying with his leg still in plaster. Shot down again in January 1943, he walked back from enemy territory. He returned to Australia in April 1943, having claimed ten and two shared destroyed and five probables, and having been awarded a DSO, DFC and Bar. He later led a Spitfire Wing in the South-West Pacific. After the war he formed a small airline in New Guinea, where he planted tea and coffee. He also collected a catamaran in England and sailed it all the way back to Australia. His autobiography, *You Only Live Once*, was published privately in 1994. (See *Aces High* and *Aces High, Vol 2* for more details.)

GILLAM, Denys Edgar, DSO & 2 Bars, DFC & Bar, from Teignmouth, Devon, joined the RAF in February 1935. In 1937 he served with a special Meteorological Flight at Aldergrove, Northern Ireland, and the following year was awarded an AFC for flying food supplies to Rathlin Island, which was cut off by bad weather. He was posted to 616 Squadron on the outbreak of war, flying with this unit during the summer of 1940, and being awarded a DFC. During September he joined 312 (Czech) Squadron as a flight commander, and then in December took command of 306 (Polish) Squadron. After a brief period off operations, he commanded 615 Squadron, flying Hurricanes on anti-shipping sorties, receiving a DSO at the end of the year. He commenced 1942 with a lecture tour in the USA, returning to form and lead the first Typhoon Wing at Duxford. Later in the year he attended the RAF Staff College, whilst in 1943 he returned to the USA to attend the Command and General Staff School at Fort Leavenworth (which I also attended later). In December 1943 he became Wing Leader, 146 Wing, in 2nd TAF, then commanding Tangmere from January-March 1944, followed by 20 Sector from April. In July he returned to 146 Wing as commanding officer and with a Bar to his DSO. This was followed by a second Bar in January 1945. He finally ceased operational flying in February 1945, leaving the service in October of that year to become a successful businessman and farmer in Yorkshire. He died there in September 1991. In air combat he had claimed seven and one shared enemy aircraft shot down, plus two floatplanes destroyed on the water. (See *Aces High* for more details.)

GILLIES, James, MC, DFM, served as a Sgt in 602 Squadron during the latter stages of the Battle of Britain. He was then posted to 421 Flight in January 1941, receiving a DFM in May after it had become 91 Squadron. He commenced a second tour in February 1942 with 615 Squadron, accompanying the unit to India in March. He later moved to 136 Squadron, where he claimed two Japanese aircraft shot down to add to the three and one shared credited to him in the West. He was posted to 79 Squadron as a flight commander, and in February 1944 was awarded an MC by the army for spotting and marking an enemy ammunition dump. He was shot down and killed by AA fire on 21 April 1944. (See *Aces High* and *Aces High, Vol 2* for more details.)

GLOWACKI, Antoni, DFC, DFM, served with the Polish Air Force from 1930, escaping to England after the German occupation of September 1939, arriving here in January 1940. He was posted to 501 Squadron, where he gained fame during the Battle of Britain by claiming the destruction of five German aircraft during a single day on 24 August 1940. After a spell as an instructor, with the classification 'Exceptional' in his logbook, he joined 611 Squadron, and then – newly-commissioned – 303 Squadron, where he served until February 1943. He then joined 308 Squadron as a flight commander, where he made his last claims, bringing his total to eight and one shared destroyed. In March 1944 he was attached to the US Ninth Air Force, flying P-51 Mustangs with the 354th Fighter Group for a few weeks. Awarded a DFC and DFM by the British, and the Virtuti Militari and other decorations by the Poles, he followed a long and varied flying career after the war, transferring to the RNZAF from the RAF and emigrating to New Zealand in 1954. He moved to civil aviation in 1958, continuing to fly until March 1980. He died on 27 April of that year. (See *Aces High* and *Aces High, Vol 2* for more details.)

GRANDY, Sir John, DSO, joined the RAF in 1931, serving with 54 Squadron and then in various training jobs, until April 1940 when he took command of 219 Squadron. A month later he moved to 249 Squadron, leading this unit during the Battle of Britain until he was shot down and wounded on 6 September. He then saw service with HQ, Fighter Command, as OC Training Wing at 52 OTU, and then as Wing Leader at Coltishall. He became station commander at Duxford in 1942, but was then posted to the Middle East, where he commanded 73 OTU. He then moved on to South East Asia, where he commanded 341 (Transport) Wing, personally dropping a Union flag and a US flag on Government House, Rangoon, on 2 May 1945, just after the departure of the Japanese. A distinguished post-war career in the RAF included serving as AOC-in-C of Bomber Command, 1963-65, whilst in 1971 he was promoted Marshal of the Royal Air Force. His decorations included CB, KBE, KCB, GCB and GCVO. Following his retirement from the service he became Constable and Governor of Windsor Castle in 1978.

GRANT, Stanley Bernard, DFC & Bar, was a Cranwell cadet who graduated in December 1938. In 1940 he served with 65 Squadron, operating over Dunkirk and in the Battle of Britain. He moved to 601 Squadron in late 1941, but in March 1942 led the first flight of Spitfires to be sent to Malta, off the deck of HMS *Eagle*. Here he took over command of 249 Squadron. Awarded a DFC in May 1942, he was promoted Wg Cdr and posted to HQ, Middle East. He returned to the island in August as Wing Leader, Takali, and in early 1943 received a Bar to his DFC. He then undertook training functions in the Mediterranean area until the end of the war. Post war he enjoyed a successful career in the RAF, becoming an Air Vice-Marshal in January 1966. He retired in June 1970, then living in France until his death on 6 July 1987. He claimed five and two shared destroyed, one unconfirmed destroyed, three and one shared probables during the war years. (See *Aces High* and *Aces High, Vol 2* for more details.)

GREEN, Charles Patrick, DSO, DFC, known as 'Paddy', was a graduate of Cambridge University and a keen skier, who also won a bronze medal as part of the British Four Man Bobsleigh Team at the 1936 Winter Olympics. A member of 601 Squadron, Auxiliary Air Force, he was called up in August 1939 and joined 92 Squadron, where he became a flight commander in early 1940. He was badly wounded over Dunkirk on 23 May 1940. On recovery he formed and commanded 421 Flight, expanded into 91 Squadron in January 1941, receiving a DFC in April. He completed his first tour in June 1941, but in November joined 600 Squadron to become a night fighter. With this unit he later served in North Africa, Sicily and Italy, claiming nine night victories, four of them in one night, to raise his total to 11 destroyed. Awarded a DSO in August 1943, he later commanded a wing of Boston bombers in Italy as a Grp Capt, also receiving a US DFC and the Soviet Order of Patriotic War, 1st Class. He left the service in 1947, and subsequently emigrated to Canada, where he died in May 1999. (See *Aces High* and *Aces High, Vol 2* for more details.)

HAINES, Leonard Archibald, DFC, from Weymouth, Dorset, joined the RAF in September 1937, serving with 19 Squadron during 1940. Here he claimed eight and four shared destroyed, being awarded the DFC. Towards the end of the year he moved to 53 OTU as an instructor, but was killed in a flying accident on 30 April 1941. (See *Aces High* and *Aces High, Vol 2* for more details.)

HALAHAN, Patrick John Handy, DFC, – 'The Bull' – was a Cranwell graduate in December 1927, with a long and quite notable career prewar. He took command of 1 Squadron in April 1939, leading us to France in September, and remaining with the unit until the latter part of May 1940, when he was posted to 5 OTU as a Wg Cdr. During the spring of 1941 he served on HMS *Ark Royal*, controlling the flying off of Hurricanes to Malta. He was then posted to the island for Fighter Control duties, but during June a group of 249 Squadron pilots got drunk and ended up in jail. He took full responsibility, and in consequence was posted to Egypt in some disgrace. Here however, he took command of 250 Wing in the Desert. However, his career in the RAF was effectively at an end, and by April 1945 he had been placed on the retired list. He died many years later in Sherborne, Dorset. (*See Those Other Eagles* for more details.)

HANBURY, Osgood Villiers, DSO, DFC & Bar, – 'Pedro' to his friends, was from Richmond, North Yorkshire. A member of the RAFVR before the war, he was mobilised in September 1939, commissioned, and joined 13 Squadron to fly Lysanders. He transferred to fighters in July 1940, flying with 602 Squadron during the Battle of Britain. In May 1941 he moved to 260 Squadron, accompanying this unit to North Africa, where he flew briefly during the Syrian campaign, being wounded by French fighters. After the unit re-equipped with Kittyhawks, he became commanding officer, seeing much action over the Western Desert. Awarded a DFC and Bar, he was rested in July 1942, but returned to the unit in November, leading it again until April 1943. Receiving a DSO, he was sent home on leave on conclusion of the fighting in Tunisia, where he got married. During the return flight in a Hudson with various other senior officers, including Wg Cdr 'Billy' Burton, the aircraft was shot down over the Bay of Biscay on 3 June 1943, and all aboard were lost. It later transpired that he had left his new wife pregnant, his son Christopher never having the chance to meet his father. During his periods on operations, 'Pedro' had claimed ten and two shared destroyed. (See *Aces High* and *Aces High, Vol 2* for more details.)

HANKS, Peter Prosser, DSO, DFC, another Yorkshireman, joined the RAF in 1935, and served with 1 Squadron at Tangmere from 1936. On return from France in May 1940, he joined 5 OTU, and received a DFC. He resumed operations with 257 Squadron in December 1940, moving in June 1941 to command 56 Squadron. At the end of the year he became Wing Leader at Duxford. He moved to Coltishall in a similar role in February 1942, but in August was flown out to Malta to become Wing Leader, Luqa. He took a very active part in the last heavy fighting over the island in October 1942, and was awarded a DSO, having brought his total of victories to 13. In February 1944 he was promoted Grp Capt, commanding a wing in Italy. He remained in the RAF after the war, becoming Wing Leader at Wunstorf, Germany, in 1948, and then serving at the Day Fighter Leaders' School until 1949. He commanded Coltishall, as a jet night fighter base, during the 1950s, and then became SASO, Levant. Awarded an AFC, he retired from the service in June 1964 and settled in South Africa, where he died on 31 January 1986. (See *Aces High* and *Aces High, Vol 2* for more details.)

HOGAN, Henry Algernon Vickers, DFC, graduated from Cranwell in 1930, winning the Sword of Honour. Initially he served with 54 Squadron on Bulldogs, and then with the Fleet Air Arm (then a branch of the RAF). In 1938 he joined 1 Bomber Group Long Range Development Unit, flying Vickers Wellesleys with the Long Distance Flight to win a World Distance record of 10,715 kilometres, Egypt-Australia. He took command of 501 Squadron in May 1940, claiming five and three shared during the Battle of Britain period, being awarded a DFC. Thereafter he undertook a range of training and administrative duties for the rest of the war, which he ended as a Grp Capt, commanding the Empire Central Flying School at Hullavington. He remained in the service, following a distinguished career which saw him become an Air Vice-Marshal in 1956. He retired in April 1962, and died on 28 June 1993. (See *Aces High* for more details.)

IBBOTSON, Desmond, DFC & Bar, was yet another Yorkshireman, this time from

Leeds. He joined the RAFVR after the outbreak of war, and first served as Sgt with 54 Squadron in summer 1941. He was then posted to the Middle East, where he joined 112 Squadron. Towards the end of 1942 he was commissioned and posted to 601 Squadron on Spitfires. By the end of 1942 he had claimed seven victories and was awarded a DFC. On 7 December he landed his damaged Spitfire on a landing ground which it transpired had fallen into German hands. Here he was captured by General Erwin Rommel's staff, meeting the general in person. However, he escaped during the night, and returned on foot to British lines. His tour ended in the spring of 1943, but he returned in March 1944 as a flight commander, receiving a Bar to his DFC in May. On 19 November 1944, having raised his victory tally to 11, he was killed in a flying accident in Italy. (See *Aces High* and *Aces High, Vol 2* for more details.)

JAGGER, John Johnstone, DFC, served as a bomber pilot during World War II, receiving a DFC whilst with 35 Squadron in 1943. He later transferred to fighters following the end of the war, and commanded 192 Squadron briefly until his death in a crash whilst undertaking aerobatics during 1953.

JAMESON, Patrick Geraint, DSO, DFC & Bar, a New Zealander from Wellington, joined the RAF in 1936. In 1940 he served in Norway with 46 Squadron, and was one of only two pilots to survive the sinking of HMS *Glorious* on 8 June 1940 when the carrier was evacuating the surviving British fighters and their pilots back to the UK. Awarded a DFC, he took command of 266 Squadron on recovery in September 1940, whilst in June 1941 he became Wing Leader at Wittering, receiving a Bar to his DFC later that year. In 1942 he led the West Malling Wing, and then in 1943 the Norwegian Spitfire Wing at North Weald. He was awarded a DSO in March 1943. After a spell off operations, he commanded 122 Wing with 2nd TAF for the rest of the war. He received Dutch and US decorations, remaining in the RAF after the war until August 1960, when he retired as an Air Commodore. He had claimed nine victories during the war. He returned to New Zealand with a CB, but developed tuberculosis as a result of his wartime experiences. He recovered from this disease satisfactorily, but died in September 1996. (See *Aces High* and *Aces High, Vol 2* for more details.)

JONES, James Ira Thomas, DSO, MC, DFC & Bar, MM, a Welshman from the Carmarthen area, joined the Territorial Army in 1913. He trained privately as a wireless operator and obtained a transfer to the RFC on the outbreak of war, joining 10 Squadron as an Air Mechanic. Posted to France in July 1915, he later began flying over the lines as an observer. Whilst serving with a ground wireless receiving station at the front, he rescued two wounded gunners under fire, and was awarded an MM and the Russian Medal of St George. He was sent back to England in 1917 to be commissioned and receive pilot training, returning to France in spring 1918 as a pilot in Captain 'Mick' Mannock's flight in 74 Squadron. Here between May – August he claimed 28 and one shared destroyed, six and one shared out of control, and a kite balloon for a total of 37 victories, being awarded MC, DSO, DFC and Bar. He became commanding officer of the squadron after the Armistice until its disbandment in 1919, then volunteering for service in North Russia, fighting the Bolsheviks. Awarded a permanent commission, he served with the RAF until June 1936. He was recalled as a Grp Capt in August 1939, taking charge of operational training for fighter pilots. During 1940 he attacked a Ju 88 with a Verey pistol whilst flying an unarmed Hawker Henley target tug, whilst in 1941 he flew on several sweeps over France, on a strictly unofficial basis. He also wrote *King of Air Fighters* – a biography of 'Mick' Mannock, *An Air Fighter's Scrapbook* and *Tiger Squadron, a history of 74 Squadron in two wars* (W.H.Allen, 1954). (See *Above the Trenches* for more details.)

KENT, John Alexander, DFC & Bar, AFC, was a Canadian who obtained his pilot's licence at the age of 17 – the youngest ever in Canada. He followed this by obtaining his commercial licence two years later. In 1935 he joined the RAF on a short service commission, serving initially with 19 Squadron. He then became a test pilot at Farnborough, gaining some fame by flying the Fairey P4/34 prototype aircraft into barrage balloon cables to test the efficacy of cable cutters in the wing leading edges. For this he received an AFC in June 1939. In May 1940 he was posted to the PDU to fly unarmed photo-reconnaissance Spitfires over Germany, moving to France with 212 Squadron in this role. He converted back to fighters during the summer, becoming a flight commander in the famous 303 (Polish) Squadron, and being awarded the Virtuti Militari by the Poles, together with a DFC. Thence he moved to take command of 92 Squadron. In early 1941 he became CFI at 53 OTU, but returned to operations in June as Wing Leader, first at Northolt and then Kenley. With his claims at 12 and a Bar to his DFC, he became an instructor again at the end of the year, then departing to the US and Canada to lecture. On return he was posted to the Middle East as a Grp Capt, where he was mainly employed on staff duties. After the war he became Chief Test Pilot at Farnborough, testing types like the DH 108 Swallow and the Avro 707 Deltas. During the early 1950s he went on exchange to the USAF, returning in 1952 to take command of RAF Odiham. He was temporarily replaced during the following summer when the Queen's Coronation Review was held there – ostensibly due to his junior status as a Grp Capt, but believed by many to be due to a drink problem which was now manifesting itself. Bitter at this turn of events, he decided not to remain long in the service, retiring in 1956 to become sales manager at Kelvin Hughes (Aviation). He remained until the company was taken over by Smiths Industries. His autobiography, *One of the Few* (Kimber, 1971) followed, but he died on 7 October 1985. (See *Aces High* and *Aces High, Vol 2* for more details.)

KILMARTIN, John Ignatius, DFC, from Dundalk, Eire, was one of eight children. His father died when he was nine years old and he was despatched to Australia on a 'Big Brother' scheme. Here he worked on a cattle station, later moving to China to join an aunt in Shanghai. He qualified as a professional jockey at one point, his adventurous life including a trip across the Trans-Siberian railway with a group of Japanese Sumo wrestlers whilst on his way to England to join the RAF, which he did in February 1937. He was posted to 43 Squadron at Tangmere, but after the outbreak of war he obtained a posting to 1 Squadron in France in the hope of more action. He claimed 11 and two shared before the unit was withdrawn, then becoming an instructor at OTU. He returned to 43 Squadron as a flight commander, claiming two further victories during September 1940, and receiving a DFC. In April 1941 he took command of 602 Squadron, and then of 313(Czech) Squadron. In June 1941 he was posted to West Africa, where in March 1942 he replaced me as CO of 128 Squadron.

He returned to the UK in August, taking command of 504 Squadron. In March 1943 he became Wing Leader at Hornchurch. After a further period as an instructor, he was posted to 2nd TAF, initially as commander of 136 Wing on Typhoons. In June 1944 the Wing was disbanded and he went to 2nd TAF HQ as Wg Cdr Fighter Operations for the rest of the European war. In June 1945 he went out to the Far East as Wing Leader 910 Wing on Thunderbolts, subsequently seeing nine months service in Indonesia. He came home in 1946 to attend the Empire Flying School, and then went to Iraq to command 249 Squadron on Tempests. Subsequently he held various staff posts in 2nd TAF and in the UK, including a period of secondment to NATO's Southern Europe HQ in Italy. He retired in July 1958 and ran a chicken farm for 15 years, before retiring to Devon where he died a few years ago. (See *Aces High* and *Aces High, Vol 2* for more details.)

LANG, Alastair Grant, DFC, served as a bomber pilot with 156 Squadron during 1942-3, flying Wellingtons and then Lancasters. After leaving the RAF, he joined Mogul Oil, where he worked for many years.

LEIGH-MALLORY, Sir Trafford, KCB, DSO, known in the RAF as L-M, joined the Territorial Army in 1914, seeing active service in the trenches on the Western Front until the end of 1915, when he transferred to the RFC. During 1916 he served with 75 Squadron on artillery observation and reconnaissance duties, becoming a flight commander. In November 1917 he took command of 8 Squadron on similar duties for most of the rest of the war. He remained in the RAF as a Sqn Ldr, becoming an instructor at the School of Army Co-operation at Old Sarum. He was to undertake various other training jobs and staff work until December 1935, when he was posted to Iraq as SASO, becoming AOC there in June 1937. He returned to the UK to become AOC, 12 Group, Fighter Command, despite having enjoyed no experience of fighters or their operations up to this point. His disputes with Keith Park, his opposite number at 11 Group, and with Air Chief Marshal Dowding, the AOC-in-C, Fighter Command, have been well-publicized. Suffice to say that in December 1940 he replaced Park at the head of 11 Group, leading this important unit until December 1942, when he became AOC-in-C, Fighter Command himself. In August 1943 he was appointed C-in-C, Allied Expeditionary Air Force, to plan and oversee the air operations associated with the invasion of Normandy. With the invasion secure and the Allied armies spreading through Western Europe, the job effectively came to an end in October 1944, and he then accepted the appointment as Air C-in-C, South-East Asia. A month later he and his wife left for India in an Avro York, which disappeared. It was not until June 1945 that its wreckage and the bodies of those aboard were found in the French Alps. (See *Big Wing: the Biography of Air Chief Marshal Sir Trafford Leigh-Mallory* by Bill Newton Dunn [Airlife Publishing Ltd, 1992] for more details.)

LEU, Rudolf Morris, DFM, known to us as 'Blue', had been born in Canada, but taken to South Africa as a baby, and then to Madagascar, from where he was sent to England for his education. In 1934 he settled in Australia, where he joined the RAAF in June 1940. Posted to the Middle East, he joined 112 Squadron in June 1941, and on 12 October he was shot down, baling out of his Tomahawk. He was picked up by troops of the Coldstream Guards and returned two days later. At the start of 1942 the squadron converted to Kittyhawks, and at this time he received a DFM and was commissioned. On 21 June 1942 his aircraft was hit and he crash-landed, suffering burns which kept him in an Axis hospital for two months. Up to that time he had claimed six and one shared victories. He was then despatched to Italy as a POW, but managed to escape in September 1943 at the time of the Italian capitulation. Unfortunately he was captured after seven weeks on the run, and was sent to Germany, to Stalag Luft III. He returned to Australia in September 1945 to become a farmer, where he died during the late 1980s. (See *Aces High* and *Aces High, Vol 2* for more details.)

LOTT, Charles George, CB, CBE, DSO, DFC, joined the RAF as an apprentice after being rejected by the Royal Navy. He was later trained as a pilot and joined 19 Squadron in 1927 as an NCO, being commissioned in 1933. He served in Iraq with 41 Squadron from 1935-38, then being posted home to 11 Group, Fighter Command. In October 1939 he took command of 43 Squadron at Tangmere, but on 9 July 1940 during a fight with some Bf 110s, he was shot down and baled out with splinters of glass in his right eye. The sight of this eye was lost in consequence, which put an end to operational flying for him. His early successes (two and three shared, and one unconfirmed destroyed) and his leadership brought him a DSO and DFC, despite this early halt to his career as a fighter pilot. He commanded RAF Hornchurch during 1942-3, then went out to the USA to supervise training of Commonwealth pilots there. He remained in the service after the war, serving as CFI at the RAF Flying College, Manby, 1950-52. Command of the Caledonian Sector of Fighter Command was followed by a spell at SHAPE in 1955, and he then became Commandant of the School of Land/Air Warfare. He retired in 1959 as an Air Vice-Marshal, and died in January 1990. (See *Aces High* and *Aces High, Vol 2* for more details.)

LYNCH, John Joseph, DFC & Bar, was a Californian who joined the RAF in 1941. He served with several units briefly, before arriving at 71 'Eagle' Squadron in 1942. In November of that year he was posted to Malta where he joined 249 Squadron. He became a flight commander in early 1943, and then commanding officer in March. He enjoyed considerable success during this period, claiming ten and seven shared, including a victory reputed to be Malta's 1,000th of the war on 28 April 1943; he was awarded a DFC and Bar. In July 1943 he transferred to the USAAF, seeing no further action. He remained in the new USAF after the war, and in 1956 was Group Operations Officer (with the rank of Lt Col) with the 49th Fighter-Bomber Wing, based on Okinawa. On 9 March that year the cockpit of his Republic F-84G Thunderjet filled with smoke, and he crashed into the sea whilst attempting to land, being killed. (See *Aces High* and *Aces High, Vol 2* for more details.)

MacDONALD, Duncan Stuart, DSO, DFC, worked as an assistant coffee planter in Kenya during the 1930s, returning to England when the plantation failed. Here he obtained a short service commission in the RAF in September 1935, joining 41 Squadron in Aden the following year. He later returned to the UK with the unit, and in 1938 became a flight commander. He was posted to 213 Squadron in summer 1940, becoming commanding officer and being awarded a DFC in December for three victories. He led the unit out to the Middle East in May 1941, where in October he completed his tour and moved to a staff job. In July 1944 he formed and commanded 283 Wing, Balkan Air Force, remaining with this unit until the end of the war, receiving a DSO in August 1945. Remaining in the RAF, he changed his name to Wilson-MacDonald on the occasion of his marriage in 1947. Thereafter he undertook various jobs, the last of which was as Air Attaché to Sweden, based in Stockholm. He retired from the service in July 1963 as a Grp Capt, and died in March 1996. (See *Those Other Eagles* for more details.)

MacDOUGALL, Ian Neal, CBE, DFC, was a Scot who entered Cranwell in April 1938. Commissioned in October 1939, he was posted to 141 Squadron, flying Defiants. He moved to 260 Squadron in May 1941, accompanying this unit to the Middle East during the following month. Here he became a flight commander and was awarded a DFC. In February 1942 he took command of 94 Squadron, which he led until May, when it was withdrawn from the front due to lack of training amongst its pilots. In May 1943 he was posted to Malta, joining 1435 Squadron, but a month later he took command of 185 Squadron, becoming involved in operations during the invasion of Sicily. He left this unit in January 1944 and returned to the UK, where he commanded 131 Squadron from May-October 1944. During his time on operations he claimed two shared victories, one with 94 Squadron and one with 185. After the war he undertook various duties, including CFI at Cranwell and War Studies Lecturer at the USAF Academy at Colorado Springs. In 1965 he was CAS, 38 Group, and then Air Defence Commander in Zambia. He served as Air Attaché in Paris, 1967-69, then retiring as an Air Commodore. He died in August 1987. (See *Those Other Eagles* for more details.)

MALAN, Adolf Gysbert, DSO & Bar, DFC & Bar, a South African, completed his education aboard the training ship *General Botha*, before becoming a cadet in the merchant marine, later serving as a deck officer. He arrived in England in 1936 to take up a short service commission in the RAF, where his earlier career caused him to be given the lasting nickname 'Sailor'. He joined 74 Squadron in December 1936, his relative maturity resulting in his becoming a flight commander in March 1939. Over Dunkirk in May 1940 he claimed several victories, whilst during the night of 18/19 June he shot down two bombers during the first major raid on the UK. For these various actions he was awarded a DFC and Bar. With the unit he continued to see much action throughout July and August, when he also became commanding officer. When the squadron was withdrawn to rest, he wrote his *10 Rules of Air Fighting* which became a Fighter Command classic, being distributed to every pilot in the Command. The unit returned to the south in October, and by the end of the year his claims had reached 14 and four shared, plus others unconfirmed or probable, the award of a DSO following. In March 1941 he was appointed to be one of the first Wing Leaders, leading the Biggin Hill Wing, a role which he continued until August, when he was posted to 58 OTU as o/c Flying Training, having received a Bar to his DSO. His total now stood at 27 and seven shared destroyed, two and one shared unconfirmed destroyed, and three probables, making him Fighter Command's top scorer of the war. In October he commenced a tour of the USA with a group of other pilots, and on his return he became CO of the CGS at Sutton Bridge, where he remained for a year, being promoted Grp Capt in October 1942. In January 1943 he returned to Biggin Hill as station commander, but at nearly 33 his combat days were effectively over. He then commanded 19 Fighter Wing and 145 (Free French) Wing until late summer 1944, when he took command of the Advanced Gunnery School at Catfoss. He left the RAF in 1946 and returned to South Africa, where he became political secretary to Harry Oppenheimer. Following the Nationalist victory in the elections, he left politics and took up farming, but later became National President of the Torch Commando Society, protesting at apartheid. He had been diagnosed with Parkinson's Disease by this time however, and became progressively an invalid, dying on 17 September 1963. There have been two biographies of this great pilot, who many consider to be the 'father' of British Commonwealth fighter aviation. *Sailor Malan* by Oliver Walker (Cassell & Co Ltd) was published in 1953, and *Sky Tiger: the Story of Sailor Malan* by Norman Franks (William Kimber) in 1980. (See *Aces High* and *Aces High, Vol 2* for more details.)

MALINS, Lionel Albert, DSO, DFC, enlisted in the RAFVR in late 1940, and was commissioned in June 1941. Posted to the Middle East, he served with 145 Squadron in the Desert, claiming two and one shared victories and two probables. Awarded a DFC in February 1944, he commanded 260 Squadron in Italy during the spring of that year, receiving a DSO in July. He remained in the RAF after the war, commanding 16 Squadron during 1948, and taking over from me as Wing Leader of the Linton Meteor Wing in April 1953. He then led the Wing during the Coronation Flypast on 15 July of that year. (See *Those Other Eagles* for more details.)

MANNOCK, Edward, DSO, MC & Bar, son of a serving NCO in the British army, was working for a British telephone company in Turkey at the outbreak of World War I. He was interned, but was repatriated in April 1915 due to ill health. In England he joined the RAMC, but a year later was sufficiently recovered to obtain a commission in the Royal Engineers, from where he transferred to the RFC in August 1916. In April 1917 he joined 40 Squadron to fly Nieuport Scouts, claiming 15 victories by September that year, for which he received the MC and Bar. He made one further claim after the unit converted to SE 5As, and then returned to England. Here he became a flight commander in the new 74 Squadron, returning to France with this unit in March 1918. In rapid succession he claimed 36 more victories and had been awarded a DSO and Bar, before being posted to command 85 Squadron on 18 June. A further eight victories followed, but immediately after being seen to shoot down his 61st and last victim, his aircraft was shot down by fire from the ground and he crashed to his death. His claims included 30 and five shared destroyed, 17 and three shared out of control, three and two shared forced down and captured, and one kite balloon. (See *Mick: The Story of Major Edward Mannock* by J.Dudgeon [Neville Spearman, 1981], and *Above the Trenches* for more details.)

MARSEILLE, Hans-Joachim, a Berliner, joined the German Wehrmacht in November 1938, training as a pilot with the Luftwaffe, and being posted to 1 Staffel, Lehrgeschwader 2, in August 1940. Seeing action over England he claimed seven victories, but was shot down four times. Whilst from reports he was clearly an engaging young man, he was still very much the rebellious teenager, and was frequently in trouble with his superiors. He was posted to Jagdgeschwader 52 at the end of December 1940, and to I Gruppe, Jagdgeschwader 27 in February 1941. He accompanied this unit to North Africa in April, where he took some time to get into his stride. By the end of August he had claimed a further seven victories, but he then mastered the art of deflection shooting, and his claims increased rapidly thereafter, adding 22 more by the end of the year. The arrival of the Bf 109F to replace the earlier E, proved to be a better vehicle for an aerial marksman, with its engine-mounted cannon, and during 1942 he claimed frequently, and usually in multiples. Promoted Leutnant, he achieved his 50th victory on 21 February 1942 and was awarded the coveted Ritterkreuz (Knights' Cross), having already received the Iron Cross 1st Class. A long leave in Germany meant that he made no further claims between the end of February and late April, but then he was able to double his score in the next two months during the Gazala battles, claiming six in 11 minutes on 3 June against Tomahawks of 5 SAAF Squadron, and six in seven minutes on 17 June, when he reached his 100th and 101st victories! Promoted Oberleutnant, he was awarded the Oak Leaves to his Knights' Cross on 6 June and the Swords on the 18th of that month. Another spell of leave called a halt until the end of August, by which time he had received accelerated promotion to Hauptmann (Captain). His most extraordinary period at the front occurred during the Alem el Halfa battle, when between 31 August and 7 September he submitted 41 claims, 17 of them on 1 September alone. This brought the supreme award of the Diamonds to the Knights' Cross, whilst on 15 September he became the third Luftwaffe fighter pilot to claim 150 victories – but the only one ever to claim such a total against the air forces of the Western Allies. His final seven claims on 26 September brought his total to 158! Two days later whilst flying a new Bf 109G over the front, he suffered an engine fire and baled out. He hit the tailplane of his aircraft as he fell, and his parachute never deployed. He was found dead, with his neck broken. Awarded the highest Italian award for valour, the Medaglio d'Oro, 'Jochen' Marseille was considered by his fellow Luftwaffe pilots to be the "unequalled virtuoso among fighter pilots". His claims appear incredible, yet it has been shown to me that over 100 of them can be directly identified by name and unit from British records – a quite extraordinary achievement. This was the calibre of the best of the opposition we were up against.

MAYERS, Howard Clive, DSO, DFC & Bar, from Sydney, Australia, attended Cambridge University in England, joining the University Air Squadron whilst there. At the outbreak of war in 1939 he was called up and commissioned in the RAFVR, being posted to 601 Squadron during 1940. He was shot down into the sea ten days after joining the unit, but by the end of September he had claimed seven victories and been awarded a DFC. Posted to the Middle East in May 1941, he took command of 94 Squadron in July. On Christmas Day 1941 he landed and picked up one of his pilots who had force-landed, flying him back to base in his Hurricane. Awarded a Bar to his DFC, he was then given command of a Hurricane Wing, but in April 1942 moved to 239 Wing to become Wing Leader, now flying Kittyhawks. On 20 July he was seen to shoot down a Macchi C202, but did not return. His aircraft was found, but he was not to be seen, and is believed to have been lost when the Axis ship carrying him to prison camp in Italy, was sunk by British aircraft. With 11 and one shared victories to his credit, he was also awarded a DSO. (See *Aces High* and *Aces High, Vol 2* for more details.)

MERMAGEN, Herbert Waldemar, AFC, joined the RAF in 1930, seeing brief service with 43 Squadron before becoming an instructor. As a highly experienced pilot he formed and took command of 222 Squadron, which he led during the Dunkirk evacuation, when he was able to make two claims. He temporarily commanded 266 Squadron during the summer, then setting up and commanding new fighter stations at Speke and Valley. In June 1941 he was sent to the Middle East where he undertook various staff and training functions until July 1944. He then returned to the UK, joining HQ, AEAF and then SHAEF until July 1945. He next became AOC, British Air Command, Berlin, followed by various other appointments. He was promoted Air Commodore in 1955, and retired in 1960 with OBE, CBE, CB in the UK, Commander of the Legion of Merit (US), Medal of Distinguished Services (USSR) and Chevalier, Legion d'Honneur (France). He died in 1998.

MOTTRAM, Roy, joined the RAF just before the outbreak of war in September 1939. He served with 92 Squadron throughout the summer, and then as a flight commander with 54 Squadron from mid 1941. He was shot down and killed over France on 31 August 1941. (See *Those Other Eagles* for further details.)

MOULD, Peter William Olber, DFC & Bar, became a boy entrant at Halton in 1933, and in 1937 was selected to attend the RAF College at Cranwell. Here, because of his Halton background, he was nicknamed 'Boy'. A great sportsman, he became a triple 'Blue' at Cranwell, from where he graduated in 1939, joining 1 Squadron after a brief spell with 74 Squadron. In France he was to claim the RAF's first victory there over a reconnaissance Do 17, and by the time he returned to England in May 1940, he had claimed seven and one shared plus one unconfirmed, and been awarded a DFC. After a spell at 5 OTU, he was posted to Malta at the end of March 1941, flying in a new Hurricane from HMS *Ark Royal*. There he became commander of C Flight, 261 Squadron until May, when he took command of the new 185 Squadron. He claimed one further victory over the island, receiving a Bar to his DFC in September. On 1 October 1941 he was shot down and killed by one of the first Macchi C202 fighters to appear. (See *Aces High* and *Aces High, Vol 2* for more details.)

O'MEARA, James Joseph, DSO, DFC & Bar, known as 'Orange', was a Yorkshireman. He entered the RAF on a short service commission in April 1938, initially joining 64 Squadron. He saw much action with this unit over Dunkirk and the UK during 1940, whilst in September he was posted to 72 Squadron, and then the following month to 421 Flight. By mid December he had claimed 11 and one shared, and had been awarded a DFC and Bar. On 17 February 1941, after the Flight had become 91 Squadron, he was shot down by Bf 109s and crashed near Folkestone, but without suffering any harm. In April he returned to 64 Squadron as a flight commander. The following year he was posted to Nigeria, but returned to become liaison officer to the Army Chief of Staff. In January 1943 he joined 234 Squadron as a supernumary Sqn Ldr, then commanding 131 Squadron until May 1944, receiving a DSO. In 1945 he was posted to the Far East, serving in India on staff duties. He left the service in 1946, but rejoined in 1950. After various courses, he was posted to 39 Squadron in Egypt in 1954 to fly Meteors, later moving with the unit to Cyprus and

Malta. Following this he was posted to the Air Ministry, where he served until July 1959, retiring as a Sqn Ldr. (See *Aces High* for more details.)

OTTEWILL, Peter Guy, GM, AFC, became an aircraft apprentice in 1931, later remustering as a pilot. In September 1938 he joined 43 Squadron as a Sgt, seeing action over the north of England and then over Dunkirk, during the first six months of 1940, when he claimed five and two shared destroyed, being Mentioned in Despatches. He was shot down on 7 June 1940 and was badly wounded, undergoing some months of plastic surgery. He returned to flying and was commissioned in June 1941, and in April 1942 became a flight commander in 165 Squadron. He then undertook the Pilot Gunnery Instructors' Course at CGS, being classified 'Above Average'; he then took command of 1490 Fighter Gunnery Flight at Acklington. Here he rescued the crew of a crashed Beaufighter which was on fire, despite being badly burned himself in doing so. For this act he was awarded a George Medal. Following various other postings, he became pilot and Air Liaison Officer to General Sir Richard McCreery, the British Commander-in-Chief in Italy, immediately after the war, then commanding 253 Squadron in that country during 1946. Returning to the UK, he commanded 257 Squadron on Meteors, whilst in 1951 he went on an exchange to Australia, commanding 75 RAAF Squadron on Vampires, then going to Korea, where he flew Meteors with 77 RAAF Squadron. Returning to the UK in 1953, he was awarded an AFC, then carrying out a number of staff functions until his retirement in 1965 as a Grp Capt. (See *Aces High* and *Aces High, Vol 2* for more details.)

PALMER, Cyril Dampier, DFC, known as 'Pussy', was born of British parents in Cleveland, Ohio, in the USA. He entered the RAF through Cranwell, joining 1 Squadron before the war. He claimed two and two shared victories during the fighting of May 1940, and was awarded a DFC. After a period as an instructor, he was posted to 234 Squadron in October 1942 as a supernumary Sqn Ldr. However on the 27th of that month he was shot down by FW 190s and killed. (See *Aces High* and *Aces High, Vol 2* for more details.)

PARK, Sir Keith Rodney, KCB, KBE, MC & Bar, DFC, was a New Zealander who served in the First War in Egypt and at Gallipoli with the NZ Artillery, being commissioned in 1915. He then transferred to the Royal Artillery, serving in France in 1916, where he was wounded and invalided out of the service. He joined the RFC at the end of 1916, initially becoming an instructor. In July 1917 he was posted to 48 Squadron to fly Bristol Fighters, rapidly becoming a flight commander and receiving an MC and Bar, a DFC, and a French Croix de Guerre, claiming seven victories. In 1918 he took command of the squadron which he led for the rest of the war, bringing his total to 20 – five destroyed, 14 and one shared out of control. He remained in the new RAF after the war, receiving a permanent commission in 1919. He was posted to 25 Squadron as deputy commander – at that time the only fighter unit in the UK. He then commanded the School of Technical Training at Manston, prior to attending the Staff College, while in 1923 he was posted to Egypt for technical duties. Returning to the UK in late 1926, he was posted to HQ, ADGB, at Uxbridge for a year, then commanding 111 Squadron. Two years later he returned to Uxbridge to HQ, Fighting Area, while in 1931 he became station commander at Northolt. He then became Chief

Instructor at the Oxford University Air Squadron, before being promoted Grp Capt in January 1935 and posted as Air Attaché, South America. In December 1937 he commanded Tangmere until May 1938, when he became SASO to Sir Hugh Dowding at Fighter Command. In April 1940 he became AOC, 11 Group, where he played a vital role throughout the Battle of Britain. In December 1940 he was replaced by Leigh-Mallory, and became AOC, Training Command. During 1941 he was posted as AOC, Egypt, and then in 1942 he moved to Malta, where again he organised a classic air defence. Finally, in 1945 he became Air C-in-C, South-East Asia, and AOC Burma. Retired as an Air Chief Marshal after the end of the war, he returned to New Zealand where he died on 6 February 1975. His biography, *Sir Keith Park*, by Vincent Orange, was published by Methuen in 1984, and republished by Grub Street in 2001 under the title *Park: the Biography of ACM Sir Keith Park, GCB, KBE, MC, DFC, DCL*. (See also *Above the Trenches* for more details.)

PEDLEY, Michael George Foxter, DSO, DFC, joined the RAF in 1935 and became an army co-operation pilot until 1939, when he was posted to instructing duties. In November 1941 he joined 131 Squadron as commanding officer, taking part in the operations over Dieppe on 19 August 1942, and receiving a DFC. He was promoted to lead 323 Wing during the Operation 'Torch' landings in French North-West Africa in November 1942, for which he was Mentioned in Despatches. Promoted Grp Capt in January 1944, he then commanded 337 Wing in Egypt, and later in Greece, being awarded a DSO in March 1945, and a Greek Air Force Cross. He remained in the service, commanding Linton-on-Ouse during 1953-4; subsequently he was granted an OBE in 1956 for operations in Malaya. He retired in 1957 and died on 9 December 1995. (See *Aces High* and *Aces High, Vol 2* for more details.)

PETERSON, Chesley Gordon, DSO, DFC, an American from Idaho, known to all as 'Pete', joined the USAAC when under age, but was released for "inherent lack of flying ability". Following this, he worked briefly for Douglas Aircraft, but in August 1940 made his way to England to join the RAF; by November he was with 71 'Eagle' Squadron. By October 1941 he had been awarded a DFC and became the first US-born commanding officer of the unit, which he led until September 1942, when it became a part of the USAAF 4th Fighter Group, and he was awarded a DSO. He became Executive and Operations Officer of the new group with the rank of Lt Col. In August 1943 he was promoted to command the group, and in October became the youngest full Colonel in the service. During his years on operations he was twice shot down into the sea, being successfully retrieved on each occasion. With eight victories and three probables to his credit, he returned to the US in May 1943, coming back in January 1944 to serve at US 9th Air Force HQ. He remained in the USAF after the war, becoming a Maj Gen in April 1965; he retired in 1968 and died in California on 28 January 1990. He had added many US medals and awards, and the French Legion d'Honneur to his decorations. (See *Aces High*, *Aces High, Vol 2*, and *Stars & Bars* for more details.)

PIKE, James Maitland Nicholson, DSO, DFC, and known to us all as 'Jimmie', was a Cranwell graduate who won both the Sword of Honour and the King's Medal. He joined Coastal Command and was flying Ansons at the start of the war, but during

1940 was posted to the Middle East, joining 203 Squadron in Aden. Here he saw a great deal of action during the Eritrean Campaign, flying Blenheim IVf fighters, and then over Iraq. He returned to the UK, where he became a flight commander in 236 Squadron, now flying Beaufighters. In 1942 he moved to 248 Squadron, returning to the Middle East to operate from Malta during the summer. Awarded a DSO and DFC, and Mentioned in Despatches three times, he ended the war commanding 220 Squadron, operating Boeing Fortress aircraft on anti-submarine work over the Atlantic. After the war he commanded RAF Kuala Lumpur in Malaya, where he was Mentioned in Despatches for a fourth time for action against terrorists. Promoted Grp Capt in 1955, he commanded various RAF stations before becoming SASO, Malta, 1958-60. He was promoted Air Cdr in 1961, commanding at Gibraltar for two years. He then attended the Imperial Defence College, before becoming Intelligence (B) at the Ministry of Defence in 1964. This led to him becoming Director of Security, RAF, from 1965-69, when he retired. He then served in a civil capacity with Naval Intelligence at the Ministry of Defence for the next nine years. He died on 23 March 1999. (See *Those Other Eagles* for more details.)

PITT-BROWN, William, DFC & Bar, AFC, was 'Bill' to his friends, but 'P-B' in the RAF. Born in Sydney, Australia, of an Australian father and a Shetlands mother, he was brought to the UK at age three, and then to Southern Rhodesia at age five. He was educated in England and entered Cranwell at the age of 18. After graduating he became an army co-operation pilot, seeing action over the North-West Frontier in India flying Wapitis in the late 1930s. He then became an instructor in India until the end of 1941, when he was posted to 5 Squadron as a flight commander, flying Curtiss Mohawk fighters. He was soon promoted to command the squadron, whilst in November 1942 he became Wing Leader of the Mohawk-equipped 169 Wing. He was sent home to England in April 1943, the voyage taking three months to complete, and here he joined SLAIS at Milfield to pass on his ground-attack experience. In February 1944, just after SLAIS had been absorbed into the FLS, and having reverted to Sqn Ldr rank on his return to England, he took command of 174 Squadron on Typhoons. He was twice shot down during cross-Channel attacks, but in August was promoted to lead 121 Wing. In October 1944 he fell foul of AVM Broadhurst, and was posted to HQ, 2nd TAF, on staff duties, remaining there until 1946. Post war he became Wg Cdr Flying at Biggin Hill in 1951, but in late 1952 he contracted polio and was badly paralysed below the waist. Miraculously, he made a recovery sufficiently complete to allow him to return to flying, and later served an exchange posting with the USAF at Langley, Virginia, as Project Officer on the F-100 Super Sabre. Promoted Grp Capt on his return to the UK, he took command of Linton-on-Ouse in 1956, but the airfield was closed down almost at once. By the time he retired from the service, he had become an Air Commodore, CBE, DFC & Bar, AFC, MBIM. (See *Those Other Eagles* for more details.)

PLINSTON, George Hugo Formby, DFC, my old 'bête noir', had attended the Royal Military College, Camberley, taking up a commission in the Yorkshire & Lancashire Regiment thereafter. He left the army in 1935 and took private flying lessons before entering the RAF. He was with 1 Squadron in 1939, but was posted to 607 Squadron before the 'Blitzkrieg', going from that unit to 85 Squadron during

May 1940, and then to 242 Squadron as a flight commander. Although he is recorded as doing some good work with that unit in France during June, it seems that he fell foul of the new commanding officer, Douglas Bader, on return to the UK, and was posted away. He then undertook various duties before volunteering for the Merchant Ship Fighter Unit in 1941. In late 1942 he was posted to the Middle East, and after a very brief spell with 3 RAAF Squadron, he joined 250 Squadron. I don't recall seeing him in the Desert, despite his serving with another unit in the same wing, but he was awarded a DFC in March 1943, then being posted to command 601 Squadron on Spitfires. Having claimed seven and one shared victories, he departed for South Africa in 1943 on a BOAC course, following which he served as a transport pilot for the rest of the war. (See *Aces High* and *Aces High, Vol 2* for more details.)

RANKIN, James, DSO & Bar, DFC & Bar, was a Scot from Edinburgh who was commissioned in the RAF in April 1935. Much of his initial service was with the Fleet Air Arm, serving aboard HMS *Glorious* as a torpedo-bomber pilot. In 1939 he became an instructor, not joining a fighter unit until early 1941, when he was posted to 64 Squadron as a supernumary Sqn Ldr to gain some experience; he then took over 92 Squadron from Johnny Kent in April. His debut as a fighter pilot proved auspicious, and between April and the end of August he claimed ten Bf 109s shot down and four more shared. He was awarded both a DFC and Bar, and on 17 September 1941 was promoted to become Wing Leader at Biggin Hill. During the next six weeks he added claims for another four Bf 109s and an FW 190. A DSO followed in October, whilst in December his tour ended, and he became Wg Cdr (Training) at HQ, 11 Group. He returned to Biggin Hill in April 1942 for a second term as Wing Leader, and by early June had increased his total to 17 and five shared plus three and two shared probables. On completing his second tour in July 1942, he received a Bar to his DSO. He then became o/c Fighter Wing at CGS until posted to command 15 Fighter Wing in the new 2nd TAF. In January 1944 he helped re-form the enlarged Fighter Leaders' School at Milfield, which he commanded. He then commanded 125 Wing during the Normandy invasion, and during 1945 was promoted Air Commodore. He reverted to Acting Grp Capt in 1946, and in 1948 became Air Attaché in Dublin, Eire. He was promoted Grp Capt in 1952, and in 1954 commanded RAF Duxford. He retired in November 1958 and returned to Edinburgh where, sadly, he drank himself to death. (See *Aces High* and *Aces High, Vol 2* for more details.)

RICHEY, Paul Henry Mills, DFC & Bar, spent part of his childhood in Albania where his father helped to organise King Zog's gendarmerie. Like myself, he also received part of his education in Switzerland, although he completed this at Downside. He entered the RAF in March 1937 on a short service commission, joining 1 Squadron during 1938. He saw a lot of action over France until 19 May 1940, when he was shot down and seriously wounded by return fire from a formation of He 111s which he was savaging. He instructed at OTU on recovery, also receiving a DFC, before joining 609 Squadron as a flight commander in April 1941. He was awarded a Bar to his DFC in July, and in August took command of 74 Squadron. During this period his wonderful book *Fighter Pilot* was published for the first time, subsequently being republished several times and selling hundreds of thousands of copies. He joined HQ, Fighter Command, in November 1941, but returned to operations on

Typhoons in 1942, first as a supernumary with 56 Squadron, and then in command of 609 Squadron. In October 1942 he was promoted Wg Cdr and posted to India where he was to command 165 Wing, but he was taken seriously ill en route. In December he took over 189 Wing instead, but was invalided home in February 1944. He then served at SHAEF until March 1945, and then at 2nd TAF HQ. He left the RAF in 1946, undertaking a number of jobs. He died on 23 February 1989, while still working on a sequel to his book. This was completed in 1993 by Norman Franks as *Fighter Pilot's Summer* (Grub Street). (See also *Aces High* for more details.)

ROBB, Sir James Milne, KBE, GCB, DSO, DFC, a Scotsman, joined the Northumberland Fusiliers in 1914, but transferred to the RFC in 1916. Joining 32 Squadron, he claimed one victory before being wounded on 11 March 1917. After a period back in England, he became a flight commander in the new 92 Squadron, returning to France with this unit and claiming the unit's first victory on 22 July 1918. By the end of the war he had claimed seven and received a DFC. Between the wars he served in Kurdistan with 30 Squadron, 1923-4, and then various other commands. He was promoted Wg Cdr in 1935 and posted to HQ, RAF Middle East. He rose steadily during World War II, becoming Deputy Commander, North-West African Air Forces in 1943, and AOC, ADGB in 1944. He then served on Eisenhower's staff at SHAPE, before becoming AOC-in-C, Fighter Command, May 1945-November 1947. He retired in 1951 as an Air Chief Marshal, and died on 18 December 1968. (See *Above the Trenches* for more details.)

ROSIER, Frederick Ernest, DSO, joined the RAF in August 1935, and in 1939 joined 229 Squadron on formation as a flight commander. Posted to France with the unit on 16 May 1940, he was shot down and badly burned two days later. He rejoined the unit as commanding officer during the summer, and in May 1941 led it to the Middle East, flying off HMS *Furious* via Malta. In October he became leader of 262 Wing, and in February 1942 was awarded a DSO. On one occasion he landed to pick up a downed pilot, but could not get his Hurricane back into the air, the pair then making their way back to Allied territory on foot, where they arrived three days later. He then went onto the staff of 211 Group until 1943, when he returned to the UK. He held a number of training and administrative jobs, ending the war as Grp Capt Operations with 84 Group, 2nd TAF. Then followed a most distinguished career with the peacetime RAF, during which he was at various times Air ADC to HM The Queen, Chairman of the Joint Planning Staff, AOC, Air Forces Middle East, AOC-in-C, Fighter Command, and finally Deputy C-in-C, Allied Forces Central Europe. He retired in 1973 as Air Chief Marshal Sir Frederick Rosier, GCB, CBE, DSO, and has since died. (See *Those Other Eagles* for more details.)

RUSSELL, Humphrey a'Beckett, DFC, joined the RAF in 1936, serving during 1940 with 32 Squadron. He was shot down on 18 August 1940 and seriously wounded, but was able to return to the unit in April 1941 as commanding officer. In October he moved to command 118 Squadron until June 1942, when he travelled out to Sierra Leone to command 128 Squadron from August-March 1943. He then returned to the UK to command 164 Squadron, first on Hurricane IVs and then Typhoons. He remained with this unit until shot down as recorded, becoming a POW.

After the war he became a Wg Cdr in October 1946, serving until 1958. He died in 1983.

RYDER, Edgar Norman, CBE, DFC & Bar, was born in India but educated in England. He served in the Royal Fusiliers, 1931-4, then became a maths teacher until 1936, when he entered the RAF on a short service commission. Posted to 41 Squadron in June 1937, he was in action throughout the spring and summer of 1940 with this unit, claiming seven and one shared. During his first combat on 3 April 1940, his Spitfire was hit by return fire from an He 111 which he was shooting down, and he was obliged to ditch in the sea, escaping at considerable depth, having watched the sea turn "from green to black". He was awarded a DFC following this episode. He was again shot down in September, but survived. In January 1941 he took command of 56 Squadron, and in July was appointed Wing Leader at Kenley, receiving a Bar to his DFC. On 31 October 1941 he was shot down by flak, spending the rest of the war as a prisoner. He was Mentioned in Despatches after the war for his distinguished service as a POW. He remained in the RAF, retiring as a Grp Capt, having commanded RAF Duxford. He then settled in the USA, where he died in 1996. (See *Aces High* and *Aces High, Vol 2* for more details.)

SANDERS, Philip James, a graduate of Balliol College, Oxford, received a permanent commission in the RAF in March 1936, joining 1 Squadron in October of that year. He left the squadron in September 1939 on posting to Hornchurch, and on 27 May 1940 became commanding officer of 92 Squadron. He left the squadron in October after suffering burns when his petrol-soaked tunic was accidentally set alight. He then served at HQ, 11 Group, until June 1941, when he took command of 264 Squadron. In 1942 he went to the USA to become a fighter test pilot at Wright Field, Dayton, Ohio. On return to the UK he joined the staff of 84 Group, 2nd TAF, serving until 1945 and being promoted Grp Capt. He reverted to Wg Cdr in 1946, then serving in Palestine, followed by Air Ministry, before being appointed Air Attaché in Belgrade, Yugoslavia, 1948-51. On return he was Wing Leader at Coltishall until 1952, when with promotion to Grp Capt he commanded Leeming. He served with SHAPE, 1955-57, and then became Air Attaché in Moscow, 1958-61. His final months in the service were spent as an Air Commodore at Fighter Command, before retirement in April 1962. He then worked for 14 years at Ministry of Defence as a civil servant. He died in January 1989. (See *Aces High* and *Aces High, Vol 2* for more details.)

SAVILLE, Eric Cowley, DFC & Bar, DFC (US), was a South African Permanent Force officer, who was commissioned in the SAAF. From October 1941 he served in the Western Desert, initially with 2 SAAF Squadron. In August 1942 he joined 112 Squadron as A Flight commander, receiving a DFC and Bar by the end of the year, followed by a US DFC. In May 1943 he was promoted to command 260 Squadron, but was killed over Italy on 19 September 1943 when his Kittyhawk was shot down by AA fire. He had by that time claimed eight victories, plus a large number of probables and damaged. (See *Aces High* and *Aces High, Vol 2* for more details.)

SKALSKI, Stanislaw, DSO, DFC & 2 Bars, was born in Odessa, Russia, of Polish parentage. He joined the Polish Air Force in January 1936, serving with 142 Eskadra as a Lt, and flying high-wing PZL P.11c fighters, he was one of the two most successful Polish fighter pilots during the September 1939 invasion, claiming four and one shared shot down. His unit withdrew to Rumania, from where he travelled via Lebanon and France to England, joining the RAF in January 1940. In August he was posted to 302(Polish) Squadron, but nine days later he moved to 501 Squadron. Here he claimed four more victories before being shot down on 5 September, and suffering burns, which kept him in hospital for six weeks. He then rejoined the squadron, but in March 1941 was posted to 306 Squadron, where in June he became a flight commander. He claimed a further five victories during the summer, before his tour ended. He commenced a second tour in March 1942 with 316 Squadron, moving to 317 Squadron in May. In November 1942 he went to 58 OTU as an instructor, but in early 1943 he joined a specially-formed Polish Fighting Team which was sent out to North Africa and attached to 145 Squadron, flying Spitfire IXs during the later stages of the Tunisian Campaign. Here he made three more claims, bringing his total to at least 20 and one shared. In July 1943 the team was disbanded and he became the first Polish pilot to command an RAF squadron, taking over 601. He had by now been awarded the Virtuti Militari, Cross of Valour and three Bars, and a DFC and Bar, a Second Bar following in October 1943 when he returned to the UK to become Wing Leader of 131 Polish Wing. In April 1944 he moved to 133 Wing, claiming his last two victories in a Mustang over Normandy during June. He received another Virtuti Militari of the higher, 4th Class, known as the 'Golden Cross' in May 1944, and also a DSO in August. In September he departed for the USA to attend the Command and General Staff School. Returning in February 1945, he became Wg Cdr Operations at HQ, 11 Group. He went home to Poland in June 1947, becoming Inspector, Flying Techniques at the Polish Air Force HQ. However, in 1948 he was imprisoned by the Communists until 1956, spending years under sentence of death for espionage for the UK and US. Partially rehabilitated, he re-joined the air force, eventually rising to the rank of General. In 1996 his autobiography was published in Polish, entitled *Miedzy niebem a picklem (Between Heaven and Hell)*. (See *Aces High*, *Aces High, Vol 2* and *Poles in Defence of Britain* by Robert Gretzyngier for more details.)

SOPER, Francis Joseph, DFC, DFM, entered Halton as an apprentice in September 1928, later being selected for pilot training; following this, he joined 1 Squadron as a Sgt. He was involved in many of the squadron's engagements from November 1939 to May 1940, claiming eight and five shared victories by the time he was posted home to the UK. He then instructed at 6 OTU as a Flt Sgt until November 1940, when he was commissioned. In June 1941 he joined 257 Squadron as a flight commander, becoming CO in September. In October, having added two further victories, he also added a DFC to his earlier DFM. On 5 October 1941 however, having shared in damaging a Ju 88 off the Suffolk coast with another pilot, he failed to return, apparently shot down by return fire. (See *Aces High* and *Aces High, Vol 2* for more details.)

SPAATZ, Carl, was known as 'Tooey', and was one of the great American air Generals. He was a fighter pilot in the first war, commanding the 13th Aero Squadron in France in 1918, when he claimed two victories during September of that year. After the war he followed a notable career in the USAAC, although in the stringent years of depression he remained in the rank of Major for a long time. During 1929, with a fellow officer who was also to reach high command, Ira C. Eaker, he established a US flying endurance record, while in 1934 he was an instructor at the Air Corps Tactical School. At the outbreak of war in September 1939, now a Lt Col, he was despatched at once to the UK as an observer, having served as a member of a special board considering aircraft supply to the Corps earlier in the year. On his return he was soon promoted Brig Gen, serving in rapid succession as Chief of the Materiel Division, then as Assistant Chief of the Air Corps in early 1941, and as Chief of the Air Staff later that year. In March 1942, now a Maj Gen, he headed a special board considering the problems being experienced with the new Martin B-26 Marauder bomber. In June 1942 he was posted to England to form the 8th Air Force, but towards the end of the year he moved to command the new 12th Air Force for the Operation 'Torch' landings in French North-West Africa, and operations over Tunisia. He was then appointed to co-ordinate the operations of Eastern Air Command and 12th Air Force by Eisenhower. With the re-organisation of the air forces in the Mediterranean in February 1943, he commanded North-West African Air Forces with AVM Sir James Robb as his Deputy. At the start of 1944 he returned to the UK as Commanding General, US Strategic Air Forces in Europe, holding this post until the end of the war there. He was then sent to the Far East as commander of the Strategic Air Forces in the Pacific, where he was responsible for organising the dropping of the atomic bombs on Japan in August 1945, which brought the war to a close.

STRATTON, William Hector, CB, CBE, DFC & Bar, a New Zealander, joined the RAF on a short service commission in 1937, joining 1 Squadron the following year. After the fighting over France in 1940 he was awarded a DFC, and became an OTU instructor; he finally returned to operational flying as a supernumary Sqn Ldr with 134 Squadron in the Middle East in February 1943, then taking command of 213 Squadron. He returned to 134 Squadron as CO in June, leading the unit to the Far East to operate over Burma. In January 1944 he transferred to the RNZAF, but remained with the squadron until May, receiving a Bar to his DFC. Returning to New Zealand, he became o/c Flying Wing at Wigram in 1945, then serving with the Commonwealth contingent in Japan, 1947-8. On return home he commanded the base at Ohakea, following which he became Air Member for Personnel and then Head of NZ Defence Staff at Canberra, Australia, and then in London. He ended his career as Chief of Air Staff, RNZAF, with the rank of Air Vice-Marshal. (See *Aces High* and *Aces High, Vol 2* for more details.)

TAYLOR, Donald Murray, DFC, entered the RAF on a short service commission in July 1937. He served with 64 Squadron during 1940, claiming two and one shared victories, but was shot down and wounded on 17 July 1940. In November 1942 he formed and commanded 195 Squadron on Typhoons, leading this unit until January 1944 when it was disbanded. He then led 197 Squadron until July 1944, being awarded a DFC. After a break from operations, he took command of 193 Squadron, his third Typhoon squadron, where he remained until August 1945. He continued to serve in the RAF until 1957, retiring as a Wg Cdr; he died in 1977. (See *Those Other Eagles* for more details.)

TEDDER, Sir Arthur, GCB, had been in the Colonial Service prior to 1914, subsequently becoming a pilot with the RFC during World War I. He remained in the RAF after the war, his intellect, ability and diplomatic skills ensuring that he rose quickly to the top echelons of the service. At the outbreak of World War II he was already an AVM in the Development and Production Department of the Air Ministry, and was to become a member of the Night Defence Committee when Luftwaffe night raids commenced. By 1941 he had been appointed Director General of Research and Development, but in May that year he was posted to the Middle East as Deputy to the overworked AOC-in-C, Sir Arthur Longmore. Within a month Longmore had been called to England, never to return, and Tedder took over. He remained in command throughout the subsequent fighting in North Africa and the defence of Malta until February 1943. Then, with the re-organisation of the air forces of the RAF and USAAF in the Mediterranean area into a single command on his recommendation, he became Mediterranean Air Commander-in-Chief with the rank of Air Chief Marshal, responsible directly to the Allied Commander-in-Chief, General Eisenhower. At the start of 1944 he returned to the UK with Eisenhower, Montgomery, Spaatz, and other experienced officers to plan and implement the invasion of Western Europe. Here he became Eisenhower's Deputy Supreme Allied Commander – a recognition of the importance of air power in the winning of the war, and of Tedder's great personal skills. Subsequently Eisenhower delegated to him direct responsibility for the co-ordination of all air operations in Europe. Following the end of the war he became Chief of the Air Staff.

TODD, Arthur George, DFC, joined the RAFVR after the outbreak of war, and on completion of his training joined 245 Squadron as a Sgt in 1941. In May of that year he flew off HMS *Furious* to Malta as a reinforcement, where he joined 261 Squadron. He then ferried Tomahawks from Takoradi to Egypt, before joining 128 Squadron in Sierra Leone, where he claimed one Vichy French reconnaissance aircraft shot down. He returned to the UK in 1942, becoming an instructor at an OTU, where he first flew Typhoons. In October 1943, now commissioned, he was posted to 56 Squadron to fly these aircraft operationally, and from there to 164 Squadron, at the time still equipped with Hurricane IVs, as a flight commander. The unit re-equipped with Typhoons, and he saw action with these until summer 1944, when he was posted to Napiers as a production test pilot. He returned to operations in January 1945 as CO 257 Squadron – another Typhoon unit – remaining here until March. He stayed in the RAF until 1958, then retiring as a Wg Cdr.

TUCK, Robert Roland Stanford, DSO, DFC & 2 Bars, DFC (US), was a South London boy who became a Merchant Navy cadet prior to joining the RAF on a short service commission in September 1935. Posted to 65 Squadron in May 1936, he remained there until the outbreak of war in 1939, when he moved to 92 Squadron as a flight commander. He saw considerable initial action over Dunkirk in late May/early June 1940, claiming eight victories here (one of them shared and one unconfirmed), and was awarded a DFC. He continued to see action over England during the summer, twice being shot down by return fire from bombers. In September he was posted to command 257 Squadron, exchanging Spitfires for Hurricanes. This did not alter his prolific scoring, and by the end of the year he had claimed a further 12 and one shared victories since August. He received a Bar to his DFC in October and a DSO in January 1941, followed by a Second Bar to the DFC in April, by which time he had claimed three further victories. After claiming two Bf 109s on 21 June 1941 he was shot down into the Channel, but was picked up safely. In July he became Wing Leader of the Duxford Wing, moving to the West Malling Wing the following month. He was then sent to the USA on a lecture tour with a number of other leading pilots including 'Sailor' Malan. He returned to the UK at the end of 1941, with a posting to lead the Biggin Hill Wing. On 28 January 1942, on a low level strafing sortie over France, he was shot down by flak and crash-landed, becoming a POW. His claims at that time stood at 27 and two shared destroyed, one and one shared unconfirmed destroyed, and six probables, plus one destroyed on the ground. He escaped from prison camp on 1 February 1945 with a Polish companion and reached Soviet lines, then accompanying the Red Army on its advance into Germany. Finally he managed to get back to the British Embassy in Moscow, and was shipped home. He was awarded a US DFC in 1946, but left the RAF as a Wg Cdr in May 1949, becoming a successful mushroom farmer in Kent. His biography, *Fly for your Life* by Larry Forrester (Frederick Muller) was published in 1956. He died on 5 May 1987. (See *Aces High* for more details.)

TUTTLE, Geoffrey William, DFC, served in the RAF through the inter-war years. He was awarded a DFC in 1937 for services as a Flt Lt in Waziristan during 1936-7. In 1940 he was given command of the PRU, responsible for all long-range reconnaissance operations over Germany. After the war he continued in the service, ultimately reaching Air Marshal rank.

URBANOWICZ, Witold, DFC, joined the Polish Air Force in 1930, being commissioned in 1932 as an observer. He undertook pilot training in 1933. In August 1936, whilst serving with 111 Eskadra, he shot down a Russian reconnaissance aircraft which had violated Polish air space. Immediately after this he was posted as an instructor at Deblin, where he remained until the German invasion of September 1939. He then led a group of 50 cadets to Rumania after the Polish collapse, and from there via France to England. Here he joined the RAF in January 1940. After initial training as an army co-operation pilot, he was transferred to fighters, joining 145 Squadron in August 1940, where he claimed two victories. He was then posted as a flight commander to 303 (Polish) Squadron, being promoted as joint (Polish) commanding officer alongside Johnny Kent. In the next month he claimed at least 13 more victories, being awarded the Virtuti Militari. In October he was posted to HQ, 11 Group, Fighter Command, and in April 1941 organised the first all-Polish fighter wing at Northolt. In June he visited the USA to recruit descendants of Polish immigrants and to lecture to the USAAC, receiving a DFC at this time. He returned to the US as Assistant Polish Air Attaché. In 1943 he went to China at the invitation of General Claire Chennault, where he flew P-40s with the US 23rd Fighter Group, claiming two Japanese aircraft shot down. He visited Poland in 1945, but discouraged by the Communist regime, he departed again, returning to Washington as Air Attaché. He was also decorated with the Polish Cross of Valour and three Bars, the US Air Medal and the Chinese Flying Cross. On release from the service in October 1945 he took up US citizenship, working for American Airlines, Eastern Airlines and Republic

Aviation. He retired in 1973, becoming an aviation security consultant until 1994. In 1995 he was reinstated by the new Polish government, and promoted to General. In May 1996 he visited the fighter unit that was a direct descendant of his old 111 Eskadra on its 75th anniversary, but on return to New York, died on 17 August that year. (See *Aces High, Aces High, Vol 2* and *Poles in Defence of Britain* by Robert Gretzyngier for more details.)

USHER, Dennis Charles, DFC, DFM, joined the RAFVR after the outbreak of war, being posted to 213 Squadron in North Africa as a Sgt in late 1942. He then joined 145 Squadron, where he was commissioned in March 1943, receiving a DFM at the same time. During this period he had claimed five victories. He undertook a second tour with 2nd TAF from late 1944, as a flight commander in 74 Squadron, being awarded a DFC. In April 1945 he took command of 274 Squadron on Tempests, leading this unit until April 1946, when he moved to 16 Squadron, remaining there until January 1948. In August 1952 he was given command of 66 Squadron, remaining until November 1954, flying Meteors and Sabres. He left the RAF in January 1963, subsequently flying for Airwork in the Middle East. (See *Aces High* and *Aces High, Vol 2* for more details.)

VERITY, Hugh Beresford, DFC, joined the RAFVR, becoming notable as a Lysander pilot carrying agents into occupied France, and flying them out again with 161 Squadron. He was awarded a DFC during 1943, at which time he was a Squadron Leader.

WADE, Lance Cleo, DSO, DFC & 2 Bars, was a Texan who became a pilot at the age of 17, but who was turned down by the USAAC due to lack of formal higher education. He travelled to Canada in December 1940 to join the RAF, and was sent to the Middle East on completing his training, flying a Hurricane off HMS *Ark Royal* to Malta, then flying on to Egypt. Here he joined 33 Squadron, achieving some notable success during the next year whilst flying Hurricanes. Awarded a DFC in April 1942, he became a flight commander in June. In September he ceased operational flying, having claimed 14 in the air (two of them shared) and one on the ground in a little less than a year. He was then flown out to join the RAF Delegation in Washington, and was loaned to the USAAF, lecturing and testing US-built fighters. Receiving news of a Bar to his DFC whilst there, he also met the President in the White House. He returned to North Africa in January 1943, joining 145 Squadron as a flight commander, but almost at once becoming commanding officer. Now flying Spitfires, he claimed eight further victories during the campaign in Tunisia, receiving a Second Bar to his DFC during March. He claimed two final victories over Italy during late 1943, plus several damaged, bringing his total to 22 and two shared, plus one on the ground – at the time the highest-scoring Allied pilot in the Mediterranean theatre. Promoted Wg Cdr, he joined the staff of HQ, Desert Air Force. On 12 January 1944, flying an Auster light aircraft, he was seen to go into a spin and crash, being killed instantly. The award of a DSO post-dated his death. (See *Aces High, Aces High, Vol 2* and *Stars & Bars* for more details.)

WALKER, G.A., known as 'Gus', was one of the great characters of Bomber

Command. A noted rugby scrum-half, he played for the RAF during the 1930s, and was a trialist for the England team. He commanded 144 Squadron early in the war, flying Handley Page Hampdens, whilst in 1941 he became commander of 5 Group. As an Air Vice-Marshal he commanded 1 Group from 1956-59.

WALKER, James Arthur, DFC, a Canadian from Alberta, travelled to England before the war to join the RAF on a short service commission in March 1938. Posted to 111 Squadron, he saw action over France, during the Dunkirk evacuation and in the Battle of Britain, becoming a flight commander and being awarded a DFC during 1940. Following a period of instructing, he joined 603 Squadron in summer 1941, but was posted to 610 Squadron in August. In early 1942, having claimed six and one shared victories, he was posted to the Middle East, where in June he joined 112 Squadron. The following month he was promoted to command 250 Squadron, which he led until September 1943. He then went to the Far East as a transport pilot, flying Dakotas with 31 Squadron from India. On 8 February 1944 his aircraft was shot down by Japanese fighters during a supply drop over the Arakan peninsula in Burma, and he was killed. (See *Aces High* and *Aces High, Vol 2* for more details.)

WALKER Peter Russell, DSO, DFC, joined the RAF in 1935, and was posted to 1 Squadron after completing his training, where he soon became a member of the squadron aerobatic team for the 1937 Hendon Air Pageant. He was the unit's senior flight commander when it moved to France in September 1939, and here in March 1940 he made the RAF's first claim for a Bf 110 shot down. During the fighting of May he raised his total to three and two shared destroyed, and two unconfirmed destroyed, and was awarded a DFC. He then instructed at OTU until November 1940, when he took command of 253 Squadron for a year. In summer 1942 he was Wing Leader at Tangmere, being awarded a DSO for his leadership during the Dieppe operations of 19 August that year. He was then posted to HQ, 11 Group until late 1943, when he commanded the CGS at Sutton Bridge, and then Catfoss; he had been promoted Grp Capt by the end of the war. Reverting to Wg Cdr rank after the war, he again became a Grp Capt in 1956, commanding Fassberg airfield in Germany. He retired from the service in March 1964, living in Devon until his death during the early 1980s. (See *Aces High* and *Aces High, Vol 2* for more details.)

WHEELER, (Henry) Sir Neil (George), GCB, CBE, DSO, DFC & Bar, FRAeS, CBIM, entered Cranwell in 1935, serving with Bomber Command after graduating from 1937-9. He then served with Fighter and Coastal Commands, being awarded a DFC in August 1941 when a Flt Lt with 1 PRU. In 1942, as a Sqn Ldr, he attended OTU to convert to Beaufighters for coastal fighter work, but before he had finished his course, he was hurriedly promoted Wg Cdr and given command of 236 Squadron, which he led from November 1942-September 1943 on anti-shipping sorties. During this period he was awarded both a DSO and a Bar to his DFC. He then attended the RAF and US Army Staff Colleges, then joining the staff of the Cabinet Office. After the war he was on the Directing Staff of the RAF Staff College and of the Joint Services Staff College, with a spell in the Far East in between (when I served with him). A fairly meteoric career followed, including a number of staff appointments and spells as SASO, RAF Germany and AOC, Far East Air Force. He was also ADC to

HM The Queen from 1957-61. He concluded his RAF career as an Air Chief Marshal in 1975, and then became a Director of Rolls-Royce until 1982, and of Flight Refuelling until 1985.

WHITAMORE, William Michael, DFC, known as 'Babe' due to his youthful features, joined the RAFVR in summer 1940, being posted to 66 Squadron in May 1941, and then a month later to 92 Squadron. He accompanied this unit to North Africa, where in May 1942 he was posted to 112 Squadron. He returned to flying Spitfires in July, when he moved to 601 Squadron. In February 1943 he joined the 244 Wing Training Flight for a brief rest from operations, returning to 601 in April as a flight commander, when he was also awarded a DFC. In July he was appointed commanding officer of 81 Squadron, this unit then being posted to India. Here he made the unit's first claim against the Japanese. In March 1944 he led a section of six Spitfire VIIIs to a strip behind enemy lines known as 'Broadway', where support for General Orde Wingate's Second Chindit Expedition was being flown in. Soon after arrival, a raid by Japanese fighters came in on the morning of 17 March; the Allied fighters attempted to scramble to intercept them, and Whitamore was seen to shoot one down before being shot down and killed himself. At the time of his death he had claimed nine or ten plus one shared destroyed. (See *Aces High* and *Aces High, Vol 2* for more details.)

WHITE, Blair Eustace Galloway, joined the RAF on a short service commission in October 1938. He served in France in May 1940 with 504 Squadron, but was shot down and wounded. He returned to the unit in August 1940, but was wounded again on 11 May 1941. He then served as a flight commander with 130 Squadron before being posted to Malta in October 1942, where he joined 1435 Squadron as a flight commander. On 3 November he took command of 185 Squadron, but was taken seriously ill with jaundice and had to give up his command. On recovery he was given command of 229 Squadron instead in May 1943, but was shot down and killed by a Luftwaffe fighter over Sicily on 5 July 1943. (See *Those Other Eagles* for more details.)

WICKHAM, Peter Reginald Whalley, DSO, DFC & Bar, was another Cranwell entrant, who graduated from the College in 1939. He was posted initially to 3 Squadron, but in September was sent out to the Middle East to join 112 Squadron. During the initial fighting with the Italians and in the First Libyan Campaign, he flew with this unit and on attachment to 33 Squadron, seeing quite a lot of action. He was then posted to 33 Squadron, going with this unit to Greece in April 1941, where he claimed three victories, being awarded a DFC in July, following the unit's return to Egypt. He then returned to the UK, where he joined 111 Squadron, being awarded a Bar to his DFC after the Dieppe actions of 19 August 1942. He was promoted to command 131 Squadron, but was then rested. In April 1943 he took command of 122 Squadron until the end of the year, when he became Wing Leader of 122 Wing on Mustangs. In March 1944 he became CFI at 2 Tactical Exercise Unit, remaining there until September, when he was posted to HQ, ADGB. He also flew on attachment to the USAAF's 4th Fighter Group, being awarded a Silver Star by the Americans. Towards the end of the war he led the Peterhead Mustang Wing, and was awarded a

DSO at the conclusion of hostilities. At this time he was said to have been credited with 17 victories, but it is believed that this was an error, and that he had actually claimed ten and seven probables. He remained in the service, commanding 43 Squadron on Meteors during 1949. Later, as a Grp Capt, he was Air Attaché in Switzerland 1956-8. He retired from the service in March 1961, and died on 29 April 1970. (See *Aces High* and *Aces High, Vol 2* for more details.)

WOODS, Eric Norman, DFC & Bar, was born in Buenos Aires, Argentina, his family returning to the UK in 1914. They emigrated to Canada in 1920, living in British Columbia, and it was from here that 'Timber' came to England to join the RAFVR in May 1940. He was placed on the reserve list until August, when he commenced training, being commissioned in January 1941 and posted to 124 Squadron in May. In March 1942 he was posted to 72 Squadron as a flight commander, and in July was awarded a DFC. He was then posted to Malta, flying off HMS *Furious* on 10 August 1942, and on arrival he took command of 249 Squadron. He was awarded a Bar to his DFC at the end of October, but ended his tour in February 1943, being posted to Egypt to instruct at 73 OTU. He returned to 249 Squadron, now in Italy, in July, whilst in November he was appointed Wing Leader, 286 Wing, Balkan Air Force. On 16 December 1943 he and Sqn Ldr K.B.L. Debenham, commanding officer of 126 Squadron, flew a sortie over the Yugoslavian coast from which they both failed to return. It was believed at the time that they had either been shot down, or had collided in cloud. Since the war it has been ascertained that no claims were made by the Luftwaffe on this date, and the latter explanation seems the most likely. (See *Aces High* and *Aces High, Vol 2* for more details.)

YEAGER, Charles Elwood, known as 'Chuck', enlisted in the USAAF as a mechanic in September 1941. He applied for pilot training, qualifying in March 1943. Posted to the 363rd Fighter Squadron, 357th Fighter Group with the 8th Air Force in England, he claimed his first victory on 4 March 1944, but next day was shot down over Southern France. He evaded capture and returned to England via Spain. Returning to action, he claimed five Bf 109s shot down on 12 October, a Me 262 jet on 6 November and four FW 190s on 27 November, ending his tour with 11 and 1 shared to his credit. In July 1945 he commenced experimental flying at Wright Field, and on 14 October 1947 became the first man officially to exceed the speed of sound in a Bell X-1 rocket aircraft. Flying a Bell X-1A on 12 December 1953, he became the first officially to fly at twice the speed of sound. He commanded two fighter squadrons from 1954-1960, then becoming Commandant of the Aerospace Research Pilot School. In 1966 he commanded the 405th Tactical Fighter Wing, flying 127 sorties over South Vietnam. Promoted Brigadier General in 1969, he became vice-commander of the US 17th Air Force in Germany. Until his retirement in 1975 he was Air Force Director of Safety; thereafter he continued to fly first line aircraft as a consultant to the air force. (See *Stars & Bars* for more details.)

ZURAKOWSKI, Janusz, attended Officer Cadet school in Deblin, Poland, from 1934, being commissioned into the air force in 1937, when he flew fighters with 161 Eskadra. In early 1939 he became a fighter instructor in Deblin, where during the September fighting he became part of an *ad hoc* instructors' defence flight. Escaping to France and then England, he joined 234 Squadron in August 1940, claiming three victories, but being shot down twice. In October he moved to 609 Squadron, but in March 1941 became an instructor at 57 OTU. After instructing at several such establishments until the end of the year, he then joined 315 Squadron. In April 1942 he became a flight commander in 306 Squadron, and then in June took command of 316 Squadron (these were all Polish units). After some time off operations at HQ, Northolt, he became Squadron Leader Flying there in July 1943. After a spell at HQ, Fighter Command, he attended the Empire Test Pilots' School at Boscombe Down during 1944. In December 1946 he joined the A&AEE at this airfield. In 1950 he became a test pilot with Gloster Aircraft, but in 1952 left for Canada where he became Chief Test Pilot for Avro Canada, testing the CF 100 fighter. He also became famous for his incredible aerobatic displays. Ultimately he tested the CF 105 Arrow prototype, but disillusioned when this was not ordered into production, he left the industry and moved to a deserted forest area, working in forestry and construction. He constructed a lake resort centre which he ran for many years. In recent years he was accepted into Canada's Hall of Fame for the aircraft industry, and to commemorate Canada's first supersonic flight, a special $20 piece was minted in 1996, featuring his portrait.(See *Aces High* and *Aces High, Vol 2* for further details.)

APPENDIX IV

CHRONOLOGICAL FIGHTER AIRCRAFT PERFORMANCE

Aircraft	Engine	Armament	Top Speed
Hawker Fury I	525 hp Rolls-Royce Kestrel IIS	2 x Vickers .303in machine guns	207 mph @ 14,000 ft
Hawker Hurricane I	1,030 hp Rolls-Royce Merlin II or III	8 x Browning .303in machine guns	316 mph @ 17,500 ft
Supermarine Spitfire IIa	1,175 hp Rolls-Royce Merlin VII	8 x Browning .303in machine guns	357 mph @ 17,000 ft
Curtiss Kittyhawk Ia	1.150 hp Allison V-1710-39	6 x Browning .50in machine guns	354 mph @ 15,000 ft
Curtiss Kittyhawk III	1,600 hp Allison V-1710-81	6 x Browning .50in machine guns	362 mph @ 15,000 ft
Supermarine Spitfire V	1,470 hp Rolls-Royce Merlin 45	2 x Hispano 20mm cannon and 4 x Browning .303in machine guns	374 mph @ 13,000 ft
Supermarine Spitfire IX	1,720 hp Rolls-Royce Merlin 66	as Spitfire V	404 mph @ 21,000 ft
Hawker Typhoon Ib	2,200 hp Napier Sabre IIB	4 x Hispano 20mm cannon	412 mph @ 19,000 ft
Supermarine Spitfire XIV	2,050 hp Rolls-Royce Griffon 65	2 x Hispano 20mm cannon and 2 x Browning .50in machine guns	448 mph @ 26,000 ft
De Havilland Vampire I	3,100 lb thrust de Havilland Goblin	4 x Hispano 20mm cannon	540 mph @ 20,000 ft
Gloster Meteor 8	2 x 3,600 lb thrust Rolls-Royce Derwent 8s	4 x Hispano 20mm cannon	598 mph @ 10,000 ft
Hawker Hunter 6	10,000 lb thrust Rolls-Royce Avon 203	4 x Aden 30mm cannon	715 mph @ sea level

OF THE MAIN TYPES IN WHICH I FLEW

Ceiling	Climb Rate to best altitude	Range	Weight Empty	Weight Loaded
28,000 ft	2,380 ft/minute	305 miles	2,623 lb	3,490 lb
33,200 ft	2,380 ft/minute to 15,000 ft	425 miles	4,670 lb	6,600 lb
37,200 ft	2,857 ft/minute to 20,000 ft	500 miles	4,900 lb	5,900 lb
30,600 ft	2,344 ft/minute to 15,000 ft	800 miles	5,970 lb	7,740 lb
30,000 ft	1,667 ft/minute to 15,000 ft	700 miles	6,400 lb	8,400 lb
37,000 ft	2,667 ft/minute to 20,000 ft	470 miles	5,100 lb	6,785 lb
42,500 ft	3,125 ft/minute to 20,000 ft	434 miles (980 miles with drop tanks)	5,800 lb	7,500 lb
35,200 ft	2,542 ft/minute to 15,000 ft	510 miles (with bombs – 980 miles clean)	8,800 lb	13,250 lb
44,500 ft	2,857 ft/minute to 20,000 ft	460 miles	6,600 lb	8,500 lb
42,800 ft	4,200 ft/minute	730 miles	6,372 lb	8,578 lb
44,000 ft	6,950 ft/minute	980 miles	10,684 lb	19,100 lb (with drop tanks)
51,500 ft	6,000 ft/minute to 45,000 ft	1,840 miles	12,760 lb	17,750 lb (with drop tanks)

OTHER FIGHTER TYPES WHICH I HAVE FLOWN ON OCCASION

Aircraft	Engine	Armament	Top Speed
Lockheed F-80C Shooting Star	4,600 lb thrust Allison J.33-A.23	6 x Browning .50in machine guns	580 mph @ 7,000ft
De Havilland Venom I	4,850 lb thrust de Havilland Ghost	4 x Hispano 20mm 103 cannon	640 mph u/k
North American/ Canadair Sabre 4	5,200 lb thrust GE J-47GE-13	6 x Browning .50in machine guns	670 mph

THE ULTIMATE

English Electric Lightning	2 x 12,690 lb thrust Rolls-Royce Avon 301s	2 x Aden 30mm cannon + missiles	1,500 mph @ 36,000 ft

When you look at this performance chart, consider particularly the relationship between engine power, weight, climb rate and ceiling. With twice the power, but two and a half times the weight, the Hurricane I managed only to match the climb performance of the earlier Fury which it replaced.

With similar power, but less weight, the Spitfire IIa and V outclimbed, had better ceilings, and were marginally faster than the Kittyhawk Ia and III – due in the main to the greater weight of the latter. Note how in terms of climb rate, the greater engine power of the Kittyhawk III when compared with the earlier Mark Ia, was more than negated by its increased weight.

OTHER FIGHTER TYPES WHICH I HAVE FLOWN ON OCCASION

Ceiling	Climb Rate to best altitude	Range	Weight Empty	Weight Loaded
42,750 ft	6,870 ft/min	1,380 miles	8,240 lb	15,336 lb
N/A	9,000 ft/minute	N/A	N/A	15,400 lb
53,000 ft	7,630 ft/minute	1,250 miles (with drop tanks)	10,000 lb	16,500 lb

THE ULTIMATE

60,000 ft +	N/A	800 miles	40,000 lb app	50,000 lb app

Note too how, weight for weight, the speed and climb rate of the jets were vastly improved over those of their piston-engined predecessors. Despite the limited time in the air, the jets also ranged further in that time because of their greater speed.

Between the first Hawker fighter I flew – the Fury – and the last – the Hunter – in a period of little more than 20 years speed had risen 250%, ceiling by 100%, climb rate by 150% and weight by about 500%, whilst armament had increased almost beyond comparison. Yet within but a few more years the Hunter had been eclipsed by the Lightning to almost as great a magnitude in most respects, other (apparently) than in armament. Even here, the presence of only half the cannons was far more than offset by the presence of two guided missiles, each capable of destroying totally an enemy aircraft at a far greater range.

INDEX